CARRIE FISHER

Shockaholic

SIMON & SCHUSTER PAPERBACKS

NEW YORK   LONDON   TORONTO   SYDNEY   NEW DELHI

Simon & Schuster Paperbacks
A Division of Simon & Schuster, Inc.
1230 Avenue of the Americas
New York, NY 10020

First Simon & Schuster trade paperback edition November 2012

SIMON & SCHUSTER PAPERBACKS and colophon are registered trademarks
of Simon & Schuster, Inc.

For information about special discounts for bulk purchases,
please contact Simon & Schuster Special Sales at
1-866-506-1949 or business@simonandschuster.com.

The Simon & Schuster Speakers Bureau can bring authors
to your live event. For more information or to book an event,
contact the Simon & Schuster Speakers Bureau at
1-866-248-3049 or visit our website at www.simonspeakers.com.

Designed by Ruth Lee-Mui

Manufactured in the United States of America

3   5   7   9   10   8   6   4

The Library of Congress has cataloged the hardcover edition as follows:
Fisher, Carrie.
Shockaholic / Carrie Fisher.—1st Simon & Schuster hardcover ed.
p.   cm.
Includes bibliographical references and index.
1. Fisher, Carrie.   2. Authors, American—20th century—Biography.
3. Motion picture actors and actresses—United States—Biography.   I. Title.
PS3556.I8115Z46 2011
818'.5403—dc23
[B]   2011024306
ISBN 978-0-7432-6482-2
ISBN 978-0-7432-6483-9 (pbk)
ISBN 978-0-7432-9849-0 (ebook)

Photo Credits
©1978 John Engstead/mptvimages.com: 80; © Alpha Library: 103;
courtesy of Dr. Arnold Klein: 68. All other photographs courtesy of the author.

For Billie and Barack,
who make my world a better place.

Despite the obstacles you've had to overcome—whether posed
by my antics or the über-unfortunate antics of the Tea Partiers
and the rest of their distressing ilk—long may you wave.

There are stars whose radiance is visible on Earth though they have long been extinct. There are people whose brilliance continues to light the world though they are no longer among the living. These lights are particularly bright when the night is dark. They light the way for humankind.

—Hannah Senesh, poet, playwright, and paratrooper (1921–1944)

Contents

Shockaholic

Before I Forget . . .

What was it I wanted to tell you?
Was it the new T-shirt-ready saying I came up with:
"There's no room for demons when you're self-
possessed"? No, that wasn't it, although I did want
to get that in somewhere and now I have . . . Oh,
yeah. I wanted to tell all you naysayers who bought
this book begrudgingly—or received it as a gift from
someone who doesn't know you that well—that

by the last page you will say to yourself (as I did), "That Carrie Fisher! I picked up *Shockaholic* expecting to read way more than I wanted to about some eager-to-please fucktard blathering on about her drug addiction and her mental illness and her poor sad life. I mean, come on, this woman made millions of dollars on *Star Wars*. What is she complaining about? She's so self-involved that they need to come up with a new word for what she is. I mean, does she have any other topic but herself? No wonder she's mentally ill. She's got herself on her mind ten, fifteen, twenty hours a day! It never ends. 'Oh, here's something about me, and here's another thing about me, and, wait, here's something about me I don't think I told you. Oh, I did? Well, here it is again in case you managed to forget it.' And the thing is, *Who's asking?* Does anyone hear any questions? I think someone actually has to pull her aside—if you can get her to shut up for five seconds—and say, 'No one has asked you a single question, not in twelve thousand years. Can't you just give us all a break? We all have lives, too, but how can we live them with her continuously blowing the lunch of her life into our existence. *No one has asked!*'

"But I truly had no idea she was so smart—and so funny! And more to the point, so *real*! I was so completely fascinated and charmed by what she wrote that by the last page I had completely forgotten that she was an over-the-Beverly-Hill mediocre 'actress' with a wrinkly neck and unsightly upper arms. And probably the most important thing I came away with is that I now have the ability to forgive myself for all those judgmental, hateful, preconceived notions that I harbored for a well-meaning person who was only trying to make me take a good, long hard look at myself by sharing her story with me, after which I said, 'Wow. I now realize for the first time that I need to love and respect others before I can truly love myself.' And by 'others,' for the most part, I mean Carrie Fisher. From *Shockaholic,* I learned that a person doesn't have to finish high school to have insight and use big words. Ms. Fisher may not be what is considered conventionally attractive—among other things her tits are so big that they'd have to add letters to the alphabet in order to identify her bra size—but it's my opinion that you couldn't find a better example of 'good people' in all of history. And, you've got to respect someone who has managed to overcome the previously unappreciated challenges of growing up surrounded by an unending procession of maids and governesses and cooks and guards, depriving her of the joys of being raised by a mother and father in a cozy house in a regular neighborhood with a dog and home-cooked meals and chores. This is a person who missed out on the ordinary, everyday essentials most people can count on as a foundation from which a sane, predictable life can be built, and who had to forge an existence for herself that made up for never having known the joy of saying, 'What's for dinner, Mom?' or 'No, I did not flush the fish down the toilet.' Instead, Ms. Fisher had to develop values in the face of the hard reality of wanting for nothing. Sure, from the outside, her life looked too good to be real—but, if you think about it very briefly, I think you'll come to the conclusion that perhaps it was too unreal to be good."

You see, even after decades of therapy and workshops and retreats and twelve-steps and meditation and even experiencing a very weird session of rebirthings, even after rappeling down mountains and walking over hot coals and jumping out of airplanes and watching elephant races and climbing the Great Wall of China, and even after floating down the Amazon and taking ayahuasca with an ex-husband and a witch doctor and speaking in tongues and fasting (both nutritional and verbal), I remained pelted and plagued by feelings of uncertainty and despair. Yes, even after sleeping with a senator, and waking up next to a dead friend, and celebrating Michael Jackson's last Christmas with him and his kids, I still did not feel—how shall I put this?—mentally sound.

So, after all this and more, you have no doubt guessed by now that I finally relented and agreed to submit to a controversial treatment that a long line of reputable psychiatrists had been urging me to consider for what seemed like centuries. With no small nod to squeamishness, I consented to undergo electroconvulsive therapy, formerly and perhaps more commonly known as shock treatment. Now, I, too, of course, believed what pretty much the entire Western world believes, thanks in large part to Hollywood's portrayal of it—I believed that this treatment was an extreme measure primarily administered as punishment to mental patients for being crazily uncooperative. But it turns out that if you're in sufficiently agonizing shape, you—or maybe not you, but, for example, I—will finally sob, "Fuck it. Let's say it even *does* turn out to be a punishment, which I doubt very much that it will, but if it did it couldn't be much more horrifically harsh than what I'm barely able to endure now, so what are you waiting for?! Go on! Do it! Do it before you don't have a mind to change."

But, as you may have heard, the main side effect of ECT is that it really messes with the part of your brain that deals with memory. What I've found is that, at least for the moment, most of my old memories remain intact, but I totally lose the months before and after the treatment. Exactly how much time I lose is really difficult to say, because what I'm ultimately doing is trying to remember how much I forgot, which is an incredibly complex endeavor, to say the least.

It occurs to me that perhaps one of the reasons I found myself sporting my enormous bulk is another by-product of that memory-addling ECT. I may have simply forgotten how to not be overweight. So, before I fail to remember anything else that could result in any future social embarrassment, I thought I would jot down a few things that I might one day enjoy reflecting on. Or, if the ECT continues to take its toll, reading some of the things I've jotted as if for the very first time. Because, let's face it, if the disastrous should occur and I fail to reduce my ever-expanding girth, I'd better have *something* funny to say. And perhaps even an insight or three. You know, something along the lines of the amusing musings of a chubby sidekick.

To paraphrase *The Onion*—and when I say paraphrase, I mean basically steal one of their headlines and change one word in an attempt to make it my own—you haven't lived vicariously until you've done it through me. So, before I forget, what follows is a sort of an anecdotal memoir of a potentially more than partial amnesiac. Remembrances of things in the process of passing.

Shockaholic

It turns out that the Italians are the unsung heroes electroconvulsive therapy—wise. It is these brilliant wise guys who gave us ECT, or as it was formerly and less respectably known, SHOCK TREATMENT. Actually, it was really one Italian in particular, though I like to think of all Italians banding together and coming up with one of the finest alternative treatments for depression and mania.

The particular Italian who brought it to us (and when I say "us" I mean "me") was a very thoughtful neurologist named Ugo Cerletti. Dr. Cerletti was a specialist in epilepsy and, as such, had done extensive experiments on the effects of repeated seizures over time in animals.

Well, we all know how crazy cats and dogs can get, and who among us hasn't had to cope with our share of nutty pigs? I can't count how many nights I've spent haunted by terrifying images of pet pigs in the throes of a seizure. Many of us are familiar with the expression, "What's good for the goose is good for the gander." Well, perhaps a lesser known saying (but certainly just as apt) is, "What's good for the anesthetized pig prior to slaughter is also effective in treating a devastated human susceptible to suicide!"

Over time, Dr. Cerletti managed to convince several other bold colleagues with sufficient spare time to assist him in developing an apparatus able to deliver brief electric jolts—at first merely to the odd crestfallen cat but eventually to actual psychotic human beings.

It was in April of 1938 that Dr. Cerletti began delivering, on alternate days, to some of the more psychotic and suicidally depressed patients, between ten and twenty ECT shocks. And you'll be happy to hear that the results were nothing short of miraculous. For example: 90 percent of the gang with everything from your wilted-garden-variety depression to hopeless catatonia showed everything from moderate to tremendous improvement! (The unhelped 10 percent were probably the agents of the improved 90.) And of course the other handy upside was that, for the most part, these patients wouldn't remember much from right before to a few weeks after their treatment, so it was rare that patients complained about the experience.

Not that, in the beginning, there weren't complaint-worthy aspects of the procedure. In the earliest days, the ECT seizures could be so violent your bones might break, especially those that were commonly referred to as the "long bones." But it wasn't long before doctors discovered a medication that could not only prevent the previously unavoidable convulsions but would also protect the longer bones of the formerly vulnerable arms and legs. Soon after, the administering of a short-term anesthesia ensured that the patients no longer even had to be conscious during those miraculously healing seizures.

Of course, ECT is rarely considered as treatment until all other valuable medications and talk therapies have failed. Then, and only then, do they suggest that you light up the dark and gloomy skies behind your forehead.

To say the least, this treatment has anything but good PR. You won't be stunned to hear that "shock" turns out to be one of those words that is almost impossible to put a positive spin on, which I'm sure is why they've done all they could to phase it out of the current official term. (Not that "convulsive" sounds all that great, or even "electro," for that matter.) I mean, come on, whenever you see ECT depicted in a movie it's pretty much always a terrifying event, like pushing someone out a window or under a train. Now, I have long been someone whose TV is on twenty-four hours a day tuned to movie channels old and new—my television is a bit like complicated wallpaper, eager to entertain but all too frequently unable to oblige. So, given the relentlessness with which I'm exposed to both the classic films and the more current offerings, I think it's safe to say I've seen pretty much all of the available mental hospital movie fare: everything from *The Snake Pit* to *One Flew Over the Cuckoo's Nest*, to *Frances*, and all the way up to *Changeling*.

Yes, even in the 2008 film *Changeling*, ECT was portrayed as the undisputed finest method available to both control and render mute the more problematically uncooperative patients in the ward. So, when doctors first proposed that I might find this treatment beneficial, there was absolutely no way on God's less-and-less-green Earth that I was going to subject myself to its reputed horrors. I, like most others, thought you had to be completely insane to consider it, or have it considered for you, and up to then I guess I didn't feel *completely* insane.

I mean, clearly no one would vote for volts until everything else had failed. It's reserved for those languishing in the suicidal ideation lounge, and I had never been truly suicidal. Not that I haven't, on occasion, thought it might be an improvement over the all-too-painful present if I could be deadish for maybe just a teeny little bit of it. You know, like a really good sleep, after which I'd wake refreshed and equal to whatever the problem had been, that problem would have now vanished.

In my first novel, *Postcards from the Edge*, my main character, Suzanne Vale, who many have pointed out bore an uncanny resemblance to me, was asked if her drug overdose had been a suicide attempt. Suzanne dismissed this notion as absurd, to which the doctor then pointed out, "Well, some might find your behavior very suicidal," to which I—excuse me, Suzanne—responded, "Well, the behavior might be, but I'm certainly not." You might even find that, with my particular combination of poor judgment and recklessness, it could be seen as being a very good impression of suicidal. It really does convince people, particularly doctor-types, and it's almost impossible to unconvince them.

My emotional difficulties were exacerbated during the period following the death of my friend Greg Stevens, whose name almost never appeared in print without the identifying phrase "gay Republican political operative." So why break tradition here? My gay republican political operative friend had only recently died, and try as I might, I couldn't help but blame myself for not having saved him. I did this largely because he died sleeping next to me (though not, technically, *with* me—see "gay") from a combination of OxyContin use and sleep apnea. But because it happened on my watch, I subsequently had a *very* difficult time putting it safely behind me. And, over time, I hope you won't find it entirely preposterous that I came to believe that my house was haunted. Specifically, of course, by Greg's gay Republican political operative ghost.

I'd heard that my home was the scene of a few spectral sightings prior to my having moved in. For example, the woman who'd lived there the longest, eight-time Academy Award–winning costume designer Edith Head, was said to roam the property on the weekends wearing a yellow nightgown. Why a woman so involved with the creation of a large number of cinema's most memorable costumes worn in some of

Hollywood's treasured films, would choose to wear something so unadorned as a nightgown—and a yellow one at that—is beyond me. Maybe she was tired of fashion and chose to wear something she could nap in for a very bland eternity. Perhaps she wore a nightgown for haunting at night! That would be a practical solution, no? But whatever the reason, if Edith did happen to roam her once-beloved home, she never floated past me. Nor did I spot any visions of Bette Davis, who sold the property to Edith, or Robert Armstrong, King Kong's captor in the original film, who built the house and sold it to Bette. No, my house was blissfully apparition-free until my gay Republican political operative (GRPO) friend Greg died in it.

Given my enormous sense of guilt, I suppose part of me *wanted* Greg to come back. In *any* form. And since corporeal was totally out of the question, ethereal would have to do. I didn't actually feel his presence until about nine months after he'd died. It was close to Christmas, and I would open the front door to the house, stand on the threshold, and call out, "Hi, Greg!" Or, "Homo, I'm Hun!" Naturally, I avoided these salutations if I thought my daughter, Billie, was anywhere she might hear me. Not to mention anyone with some authority to have me committed.

At some point around this time, I was conferring with my book editor, and when I mentioned feeling Greg's GRPO energy around the house she recommended I call the author of a book she was editing, who coincidentally also happened to be a psychic and who she felt might be able to shed some light on my recent darkish times. I did finally phone the woman, who told

me that she felt that the reason Greg might still be around—
and as I said, in my opinion, he was *very* around—was because
he hadn't realized yet that he was dead. He had been yanked
from the world so suddenly that he didn't know that he was no
longer still in it. I told her that I felt that for quite some time
now the air in the house seemed saddled with something more
complicated than air. And I wasn't the only one who felt that
heaviness, either. A lot of people staying with me at the time
had told me that they felt something, too. Okay, so maybe not
all these people were safely on the sober side, but I'd spent a
shitload of time in my life more than slightly shitfaced and not
once was I ever troubled by spirits—alcoholic or otherwise.
Over the next six months, this Greg-ish feeling diminished until
one day I noticed it had gone away entirely. Perhaps he finally
realized he wasn't alive anymore.

But in my stressed state—oh, no! Unfortunately oh, yes!—
I had begun using drugs again. And not just any drug. No, I
had to start using the drug that Greg had so recently done to his
premature death. I began snorting OxyContin.

Now, I am not a stupid person. I'm a fairly intelligent person who does stupid things. Incredibly stupid things. I can't
defend it. I can explain it until the end of time, but that still
doesn't make it in any way excusable, especially when you factor in the impact it had on my daughter (along with anyone
else in my bonkers life who gave a shit about me). And I did it
knowing full well how painful it was to have a parent who was
unable to resist the impulse to resort to getting consistently altered. Altered and unavailable.

Back when Greg died, the first thing Billie said to her father was, "Now Mommy will be sad." She didn't express how having a dead friend of ours affected *her* directly. No, she immediately considered what his death would do to *me*, and perhaps secondarily how difficult, eventually over time, my grief and guilt would be for her. I tried really hard to make it not matter. Truly, I wanted so badly to be okay. Sure, yeah, for myself; but more than that for her. To protect her from the darker parts of me.

But I failed. It's difficult to put into compelling words the sort of toll it took on us both. I tried—I swear, I tried—to pull myself up by my bootstraps and get on with my life. But (a) I don't wear boots (so pulling up their straps was out) and (b) I found I simply couldn't.

I tried to take a version of the AA wisdom to heart. "What others have done I can do." I found myself watching documentaries of World War II veterans describing the horrors they'd barely survived, and their tragedies humbled and weirdly consoled me. My experience of Greg's death, my blaming myself for his loss, or however you want to describe it, was a freckle on the esophagus of what these men had gone through. I figured that if these guys could get through *that*, then surely I could overcome my measly dark feelings. But, unfortunately, not without that detour through my dear old hunting grounds, dope. (And what a good word for it that is.)

At some other point during my intermittently self-destructive existence, I heard someone's counselor say, "If it wasn't for drugs and alcohol, a lot of us would've killed ourselves." I thought about that as I ingested my Oxy, abusing this insight as a justification for needing to mute the large sound of Greg's fallen tree. Of course, I should have gone to a grief counselor and/or to meetings—both of which I eventually did—but first I bungled through this not-so-shortcut.

No wonder I felt Greg's ghost haunting me, right? I summoned the guy every time I took in the comfy poison that blurred him almost all away. So eventually—as it always, always does—it all caught up with me. Those around me began considering how and when best to intervene. Coincidentally, the moment they chose was the very day that I'd decided to turn myself quietly in to the authorities. But too late! Just as I was about to surrender to the psychopharmacologists, the addiction doctors, and the reliably saving grace of Twelve Steps, a few of my friends phoned Billie's father and confirmed what he no doubt already suspected—that I was high, and as a result, my mothering skills were tragically very low.

Boy, was I beyond pissed at them! Newly sober and righteously indignant (which puts the "duh" in redundant), I began referring to my intervenors as the heavy meddlers. Why hadn't they called me before calling Bryan?! Blah, blah, blah . . . all of which I'm beyond ashamed of now, and which eventually resulted in my sitting down and writing more than a few amends letters, belatedly assuring them I understood they'd acted in my—but more to the point, in Billie's—best interest. They'd done what they did out of love for me and concern for my daughter. But oh, the months it took to get me to the letter-writing place! You know the one, a few miles beyond all that indignant self-righteous narcissism. The time it took for me to come to my recently and all-too-willingly abandoned senses was a period I wouldn't return to for the world. And the whole wide one at that.

So, while I underwent that long demoralizing return trek to my version of normal, Billie went to live with her father, which was obviously the move that made the most sense, given that I was not only not any longer a person she could in almost any way rely on, but was also no longer anyone whose gestalt was anything predictable or reassuring. But simply because this was the most sensible solution under the circumstances didn't do much to make my loss of her treasured company any easier to bear. For the first time in my life I really felt that I understood the word "heartbroken." Which, of course, was made all the worse by knowing that I had brought all this breakage on my-self. But she would remain safe and out of my potential harm's way until I could turn my insensibly spinning life around.

Having betrayed Billie's trust, I had to find my way back to being someone she could once again believe in. I had to try to recover whatever I could of what I'd previously heard re-ferred to as a "maternal instinct." I had to prove—not only to my daughter but to anyone else who had managed to maintain some sort of closeness to me other than proximity—that the management (that is, the diminishment and rearrangement) of my selfishly precious fucking feelings was not the sole or all-too-primary purpose of my misguided life.

I wish I could explain—and armed with that explana-tion, somehow excuse—the seemingly unending, ongoing, relentless, inordinately intense, pathetic fixation I have with my *feelings*. That wilderness lurking somewhere down south in my bi–solar plexus and, simultaneously, right there in back of my eyes, demanding my attention and eternally taking my emotional temperature. How do I feel? No, really *how do I feel?* How *could* I feel? Some other way, surely. By the end of this endless archeological self-examination, the observer part of your mind doesn't know what it's looking at anymore. Because being both archeologist *and* pit is, essentially . . . don't make me say it . . . oh fuck. Okay . . . The pits.

As luck wouldn't have it, all this coincided with the exact moment that I was scheduled to take my show on the road. And that is *not* a euphemism for anything. *Wishful Drinking* was actually booked into the Berkeley Repertory Theatre for a two-month run in early 2008. And the only thought going through my head, pretty much 24-7 then, was, "My daughter hates me." Well, that and, "I'm hungry for fattening food."

There I was getting up onstage every night, delighting people with my hilarious life story and sharing all this perspective and insight that I'd gained by circling the drain and such, and if people had known how I really felt, I'd have been nominated for an Oscar for Best Actress even though I wasn't in a film or portraying a character other than my measly aging self. I don't know how I got through it. Or maybe I didn't get through it, but either way I was a mess.

Offstage, I couldn't put things into words, and that was the one thing I'd always been able to rely on. Putting my feelings into words and praying they wouldn't be able to get out again.

It had always been my salvation. If I could get it into words, I could escape the slow quicksand of almost any bad feeling, but now I'd lost my ability to even do that. I was in pain squared, pain cubed, pain to the *nth* power. And this wasn't the more noble sort of pain—this was that embarrassing pain of self-pity because I truly believed that Billie would never be able to forgive me. And so naturally I would never be able to forgive myself. She hated me, and I just knew she hated me, because she had every right to hate me. *I* hated me. Join the crowd! It was a trend!

I started seeing this child psychologist to help me help Billie through this, and one afternoon at the conclusion of our session, she studied me briefly and said something like, "You know, I hope you're not considering some sort of self-harm or suicide, because that would be *really* bad for Billie." So, see? She *was* helpful, because that would *never* have occurred to me.

By then, it won't stun you to learn, I was truly ready to try anything. Someone could even have recommended a therapy where you just climb into a big vat of dyslexic snakes, or a therapy where they cover you with orange sherbet and drizzle maple syrup on you—*anything!* But, no, what they suggested was electroconvulsive therapy, and I must have said, Why not?

At that point I didn't know anyone who'd ever undergone this treatment. Oh, sure I remembered hearing a woman talk about it in her clearly audible voice during her brief stay in a mental hospital back east. This pale, gaunt depressive told our little damaged group, "I was planning to kill myself, but then I thought, 'Well, okay, I can always do that, I definitely have that option, but maybe first I'll try this ECT thing. And then if that doesn't work, *then* I can kill myself.' " It occurred to me that was its place in the pantheon of remedies—the last resort for those people whose only other options are the taste of a gun barrel, a long hard fall, a carful of carbon monoxide, an overdose, or a noose.

Happily, none of the stories I'd previously heard about ECT turned out to be true anymore. Spoiler alert: You're given a short-acting anesthetic and a very effective anticonvulsant, you go to sleep for about ten minutes, and your big toe moves a bit, which is all that remains of the bone-snapping thrashing of old.

I've found that people are especially curious about how I was convinced to submit to a treatment I'd spent my entire life regarding as tantamount to torture. What was said that enabled me to finally agree to let them put their little nicotine-patch-looking things on either side of my head? And the answer is, I don't remember. *I don't*. I've found that the truly negative side effect of ECT is that it's incredibly hungry and the only thing it has a taste for is memory. I can't begin to tell you how many friends have asked me what it felt like waiting for that first shock, and all I could answer was, "You know what? I seriously can't remember a fucking thing. For all I know, they could have dressed me in a ball gown, surrounded me with dancing dolphins, and married me off to Rush Limbaugh."

But, after doing it a few dozen times, you gradually find yourself able to recall and even describe the experience. The nurses lay you gently down on a gurney. Then these attendants wheel you over next to a doctor standing in front of what essentially looks like a record player—something about the size of a small television. Then the doctor puts cute little sticky pieces of film that are attached to wires on each side of your forehead. And then, who should merrily materialize at your side but the trusty anesthesiologist, and as he starts the injection, he says something reassuring like, "Now dream a nice dream."

So I attempt to oblige him and maybe fifteen minutes later, I wake and trade in my backless gown for my street (Rodeo Drive) clothes and take the elevator back to the underground parking lot, where I get in my car and lie down in the back seat, and someone who hasn't just had significant amounts of electricity sent howling through his head drives me home, where I sleep for the next three or four hours.

And whereas before my brain had felt as though it was set in cement, leaving me . . . I don't know . . . kind of stuck, the ECT blasted my Hoover Dam head wide open, moving the immoveable.

In the beginning, they did it three times a week for three weeks. Eventually we settled into once every six weeks—which is where we've set down roots and stayed. And, over time, this fucking thing punched the dark lights out of my depression. It did for me what drugs had done for me. It was like a mute button muffling the noise of my shrieking feelings. Your whole life you hear about this terrifying treatment that turns you into a vegetable, only to finally find out that it had all the charming qualities of no big deal. Sort of like getting your nails done, if your nails were in your cerebral cortex.

So here I am, on maintenance now, and for now, at least, here I intend to stay. I go in for a tune-up whenever I notice the onset of depression, which I frequently don't recognize until it's within earshot of too late. Sometimes a few weeks might pass until I say, "Oh, wait! Shit! I don't think I've changed clothes in maybe five days." Then I might start to feel like doing drugs would maybe be a sensible idea, and that right there is pretty much the clincher.

But did I tell you that this thing is a bitch on memory? Probably, but it might be worth repeating. I mean, let's say, I read an e-mail—"That was a fantastic dinner the other night. Thank you so much"—and I have absolutely no clue who wrote it, what we ate, or where we ate it. Anybody I'd met during that first intense blast of silent shock is gone. Everybody. In a way, you don't tend to forget old memories so much as you lose the ability to generate new ones.

What I've noticed recently is that ECT doesn't remove entire chunks of memory so much as little bits of it. It's sort of like, I don't have too much trouble remembering events, but what I now lose are words, and sometimes they're really basic ones, which can be pretty embarrassing, so I'm not really a big fan of that. And I'm not talking about obscure words here. These can be ones that you might really need a lot. You know, whereas before I might occasionally lose words that anybody might misplace—like "pastiche" or "schadenfreude" or "Luddite"—now I can even lose more practical words, and I lose them a lot. For example, "practical." I can lose that word, and I'll be fumbling, "Um, uh," looking for it everywhere and I don't even get close. So whoever I'm talking to might end up fumbling around *with* me, and chances are they'll find the word a lot sooner than I will. And when they do, it turns out that I haven't even gotten remotely near it. Sure, I know the feeling of the word and I might even be able to locate one with the same amount of letters or syllables, but there's no way in hell I'm going to get near the fucker, because I've lost all the energy or enthusiasm for the hunt. It becomes not worth it. You know, how much rummaging around can you do to find this word you're only going to use occasionally at best?

The bottom line is that my vocabulary has taken a real hit, leaving me perhaps not that eloquent anymore. Then again, plenty of people probably thought I sounded more pretentious than eloquent anyway, right? Like a carhop who swallowed a dictionary. So see? There might be an upside to all this, like maybe now I'm more plainspoken. Or maybe I just *sound* more plainspoken (but I break just like a little, absentminded girl).

But since I expect to have a bad memory now, I pay extra attention to things, as if there's going to be a pop quiz about my life at the end of each day. What do I recall about what I did? So I try to make a point of remembering things while they're happening.

Of course my memory loss could as easily be caused by my drug intake over the decades that began with my late teens, or by aging, as by the electroconvulsive therapy (or a combination of all three—or as I'm fond of saying, LSD, AGE, & ECT). What I do know, though, is that my memory is a lot worse since the treatments. But, hey, it could just be that I'm remembering this whole thing wrong.

Ultimately, though, who gives a shit why I can't remember what I can't remember when I feel so much better, right? I mean, it's not as if I've been putting my purse in the refrigerator or anything. I mainly just forget people's names, some of whom I've known most of my life. But this was something I was always capable of doing anyway, only now it's worse. Hey, even if I *can't* remember their names, I'm still mighty glad to see them! And if they appear to be in trouble I can always yell, "Hey! Look out!" And chances are, if they're not deaf, they'll move before that sinister clown stabs them or the piano falls on their head.

Another thing is that I find myself forgetting movies and books, some of which I only recently enjoyed, which, if you think about it, is really not *that* bad, because now I can be entertained by them all over again. And grudges? How can you hold on to something you don't remember having to begin with! All of which has the potential to make me a nicer, kinder, far less affected human being. Someone more equipped to live in the present, now that the past seems to be otherwise engaged.

The prelude to all of this ECT business was to take pounds of medication, which aided me in my determined quest to gain tens of thousands of pounds of weight. So my medically induced mood improvement made me look fat and awful, which resulted in my getting depressed again. So who would you rather be with? Unplugged Carrie, fat and weeping torrents of medicated tears, or plugged-in Carrie, forgetful but fine-ish, and on the right side of plump? You choose. No, wait! It's my life. I'll choose. One could argue that, by having regular ECT treatments, I'm paying two—that's right, two—electric bills. One for the house and one for the head.

Ultimately, I think what all of these jolts of electricity are doing is helping to blast me to the end of any unhappiness that is not situational. I mean, really, what other explanation is there? You have to figure that there's a limit to pretty much everything. With the possible exception of certain beyond-belief reality shows, how long can something go on, right?

Wishful Shrinking

You know the saying, "You're your own worst enemy"? Well, thanks to the Internet, that's no longer true. It turns out that total strangers can actually be meaner about you than you ever could amazingly be about yourself. Which is saying a huge amount with me, because I can really go to town hurting my own feelings. I know where they are.

I Googled myself recently (without a lubricant, which I really don't advise) and I came across this posting that said, "What ever happened to Carrie Fisher? She used to be so hot. Now she looks like Elton John." Well, this actually did hurt my feelings—all seven of them—partly because I knew what this person meant. But as I'm fond of saying, "As you get older, the pickings get slimmer, but the people sure don't."

Yes, it's true. All too true. I let myself go. And where did I go to? Where all fat, jowly, middle-aged women go— refrigerators and restaurants (both fine dining and drive-thru). To put it as simply as I possibly can and still be me: Wherever there was food I could be found lurking, enthusiastically eye-ing the fried chicken and Chinese food and pasta. Not to men-tion the cupcakes and ice cream and pies, oh my!

How could I have allowed this to happen? What was I thinking? More to the point, what was I *eating*? And having eaten it, why did I eat so much of it? And having eaten that much, why did I so assiduously avoid aerobics?

I bravely mustered the long-overdue nerve to literally stand on a scale and while upright, albeit intimidated, confronted my actual unbelievable weight. Of late and for too long I had been making people—doctors, nurses, pimps, stylists, and such— keep my obese(ish) update from me for the better part of an otherwise pretty bad year. I'd been assuming that I was "only" forty pounds above my ideal weight, but it turns out that the actuality was tragically closer to sixty. Way closer. And when I say way, I mean *weigh*.

What I didn't realize, back when I was this twenty-five-year-old pinup for geeks in that me myself and iconic metal bikini, was that I had signed an invisible contract to stay looking the exact same way for the next thirty to forty years. Well, clearly I've broken that contract. Partly because, in an effort to keep up my disguise as a human being, I had a child at some point. And then, in an effort to stay sane for said child, I took pounds and pounds of medications that have the dual effect of causing water retention (think ocean, not lake) while also creating a craving for salad—chocolate salad. So yes, in answer to your unexpressed question, sanity *does* turn out to come at a heavy price.

And finally almost a year ago I perhaps inexcusably quit smoking—a famously fattening form of self-improvement whose reward was my being taken over by the famously challenging urge to hurl heaps of non-nutritious nourishment into that hole in my head under my nose. You might say (if you were Henny Youngman and had nothing else to do) that I was throwing good calories after flab. Anyway, before long I left my single-digit-sized slacks eating the dust in my closet's rearview mirror in favor of leggings. You know, the ones that give and stretch to accommodate one's ever-widening Sequoia-sized thighs. So I sported the leggings below and what was tantamount to a giant tea cozy above, my fashion statement basically being, "I'm sorry." ("Hey," Henny Youngman yelled at me from across my life, "whatever floats your bloat!" What a *jerk*, right?)

So, until I hopefully managed to get it replaced, the photo on my Wikipedia entry was grotesque albeit accurate. I can only imagine it was put there by someone who hates me and has too much time on his or her hands. I don't know, maybe it was just one of those über-accurate pictures of someone—myself, say?—situated precariously past her fiftieth year and languishing in very unflattering lighting while being captured, for all time and for everyone with Internet access, in that flattering angle *under her jaw,* causing me to look not so much like someone with a double chin as someone whose neck starts at her lower lip and continues straight to her alphabet-resistant monster rack. It might just be that my jaw drowned. It was last seen lounging precariously between my face and neck, keeping them apart for pity's and safety's sake, and the next thing I knew I was one long head from hairline to treasured chest.

I've always wished that I was someone who really didn't care what I looked like, but I do. And yet, even though I end up caring about it almost more than absolutely anything, it takes way more than a lot to get me to do anything about it. So, wide bottom line, I would rather stay in my house, unnoticed and ashamed, than go out and subject other people to having to think of something nice to say to me like, "I like your shirt." Or, "You look so . . . *healthy!*" Rather than hearing someone I respected until that moment lie to my fat face and say, "Wow, you're looking good!" and rather than subject us all to hidden painful social experiences like this, I remained behind closed doors.

Now, I've always heard that one of the most important things in life is to be comfortable in one's own skin. Well, I may have unconsciously come to the not illogical conclusion that the more skin you have, the more comfort you'll feel! Presumably you've heard of making a mountain out of a molehill? Well, that once fussy molehill was now this eternally black-clad mountain. And, if my alleged resemblance to Elton John turns out to be a problem for anyone out there, all I can really say (politely and in a sing-song voice) is "blow my big bovine, tiny dancer cock!" Or you could just skip the whole thing—your choice.

Anyway, I finally reached the point where *nothing* in my closet fit other than a few socks, some hats, and a scarf. Ultimately it might just as well have been an entire other human's closet. Basically, I was drifting closer and closer to that point of no return where one has to buy two seats on an airplane and/or their families are forced to bury them in grand pianos.

But come the fuck *on*, how many women do *you* know who are over forty-five, or over fifty—and don't get me started on over *fifty*-five—how many women of this ever-advancing age do you know who are effortlessly lean and impishly lithe? Oh sure, I'd be thin, too, if I starved myself and spent a tragically huge portion of the day jogging and/or hurling myself ever forward, drenched in sweat and downward dogging my sunrise salutations, before moving on to Pilates sessions filled with far-from-free weights. Sure, if I did all that, it would be virtually impossible to *not* resemble a busty clothespin. But to be a feast for an army of snacking eyes requires devoting enormous chunks of your time to denying yourself on the one hand and forcing yourself on the other.

There's a breed of women in Hollywood who wander among us looking very tense and very mad. Of course they're angry. Who wouldn't be enraged about having to ensure you're looking an age you haven't been in a generation? Regarding the concept of letting yourself go, shouldn't we be able to at some point? Of course, whether or not we *should* be able is moot. There are two choices post forty-five: letting ourselves go or making ourselves sit like good, well-groomed, obliging pets, coats smooth and wrinkle-free, stomachs flat, muscles taut, teeth clean, hair dyed, nails manicured—everything *just so*. The thing is, though, not only is this completely unnatural, requiring warehouses full of self-control and perseverance, but it demands a level of discomfort you have to be willing to live with 'til death by lap band or liposuction. Until then, everyone marvels at how almost *completely* unengaged you look! It's spooky. You look like a teenager! To the point where I kind of want to ground you. "Go to your room! Because I *said* so. And no dinner!"

People spend oceans of time ensuring that they are camera ready at all times. They glide through this unofficial American-Idolized world aching to impress the *very* judgmental audience that we move among, inspiring them to say, "No! I don't believe it! You *can't* be. I could have *sworn* you were *sisters!*

You *must* tell me your secret! *Please!*" Because given a choice between youth and beauty or age and wisdom, I'll let you guess which one most of us would opt for. Take all the time you need. I'll wait here . . .

Then, just when I'd almost resigned myself to living out my remaining years as Betty the fat girl, my unexpected ship came in, the S.S. *Jenny Craig.*

I mean, is this an amazing planet or what? There I am, ginormously minding my own business—show, monkey, and otherwise—when where should I suddenly find myself but right up there in lights on none other than Jenny Craig's list!

That's right. I am getting paid to do something I ought to have done years and years and pounds and pounds ago.

Now, before you think, *Sure, just because she's a celebrity she gets all the breaks while all the noncelebrity* . . .

Hang on. Before you go any further, don't forget—not only do I win the wacky Jenny Craig lottery, I'm also a bipolar recovering addict who woke up next to a dead friend after getting left for a man—these and a few other such shrink-employing events could be seen, from a certain vantage point, to kind of balance out the Jenny eat-less luck fest.

Of course the Jenny Craig folks are always on the lookout for giantly fat celebrities to go on their program and prove how easy and effective it is. And I was humiliated—being the poster girl for enormousness is not something any kid grows up aspiring to.

And though much of this makes me a whore of giant proportions, I also wouldn't be a whore with just *any* John. See, I'm not that good a liar. I mean, there's a lot of other things I could do for money. I could sell autographed ECT machines or rhinestoned mood stabilizers or even *Star Wars* scented laxatives. But do I do that? Do I do a commercial on television to (attempt to) sell a medication while running around some random backyard with some rented golden retriever laughing and looking cured and totally amazed to be so worry-free while a voice comes on and says, "Reginol is not recommended for wayward fish or Libras with dementia. If you notice swelling in your femur or notice a subtle beam of backlight glowing northward from your anus or the anus of someone you went to school with, call your doctor immediately as this could be a symptom of hydrocephalus that could lead to roughhousing and misguided bloat. Reginol is not recommended for pregnant Nazis or yodelers over seventy. Reginol does not protect you from unpopularity or autism . . ."

All I'm ultimately saying is, how great is it that I've been paid handsomely to get healthy and weigh what people have to weigh to be pretty? Or pretty thin. In any event, this is a fuckin' awesome confluence of debt reduction and cutting my swollen self down to social life size.

Craig is great,

Craig is good,

Thank you for this portion-appropriate food. A-men!

And by "men" I mean the four or five that might look at

me again in a few Jennified months. And when I say look, I don't just mean in amazement at my vague resemblance to a space princess from the silent screen era, but because I look good for *my* age, and maybe even for the age I was a year or two ago.

The Senator

What else was I going to tell you?
Oh, yeah! About the time I went on a blind date with
a senator from Connecticut. (No, sorry, it wasn't Joe
Lieberman.)

In 1985, I was filming a TV miniseries—a now
almost quaint form of entertainment (currently being
singlehandedly kept from extinction by HBO) that
unspooled its yarn over a contained period of several

life-altering nights. This particular miniseries, which set out to tell the story of how the Frenchman Frédéric Bartholdi came to build the Statue of Liberty, answered to the imaginative name of . . . wait for it . . . *Liberty.* It starred, among others, Chris Sarandon, Frank Langella, Dana Delany, LeVar Burton, Claire Bloom, George Kennedy, and me. I played Emma Lazarus, the gal whose sonnet, "The New Colossus," appears on a plaque on Lady Liberty's base: "Give me your poor, your tired, your huddled hunchbacked masses yearning to be free, fun-loving, and straight-backed—or, if not actually straight, then gay, as befits an immigrant mincing stylishly through Ellis Island." I may be misremembering some of the words, but hopefully you get the gist.

Liberty was shot on location in Baltimore, a semi-stoned throw from Washington, D.C. At some point while the weeks of filming marched majestically monthward, a producer friend from L.A. suggested that I look up Chris Dodd, who, in addition to being his buddy, was also a U.S. senator.

At the time I had become less discriminating than I might have been about the projects I subjected myself—as well as a potentially agonized audience—to. Not quite thirty, my filmography included not just *Shampoo, Hannah and Her Sisters,* and the *Star Wars* trilogy, but also such seminal classics as *Hollywood Vice Squad* (I played a policewoman out to take down a child pornographer) and *Under the Rainbow,* considered to be the *Gone With the Wind* for the under-four-foot-six set. (One review described it as "a 'what-if?' comedy that poses the question: 'What if 150 people auditioning to play the Munchkins in MGM's *The Wizard of Oz* were staying in the same hotel as some Nazis and a group of spies?'") If you look it up on the Rotten Tomatoes website, you'll find this prominently displayed excerpt from that review: "A peculiar career choice for Fisher."

Liberty, though, had some class. I mean, it was written by Pete Hamill, which was nothing to sneeze at, right? (And where does this phrase "nothing to sneeze at" come from, and why is it such a negative? I often consider sneezing at things as a tribute of sorts.) So, having recently graduated completely healed and normal from my first stint in a rehab, and appearing in an almost perfectly respectable piece of work, I found myself driving from Baltimore to Washington, D.C., to have dinner with Chris Dodd, this senator who I knew virtually nothing about.

Nor did Senator Dodd—like most people, then, now and always—have any idea who I was in the wide, wide world beyond this cute little actress who'd played Princess Leia. And, what did it matter? That *is* who I was. Maybe not to myself, but then I won't be consulted on that future day when my death is reported and a picture of Princess Leia will appear on television with two dates under my absurdly bewigged face.

The senator was not a handsome man, but he was far from unattractive. Probably in his early fifties, he had, as I recall, the reddest of cheeks, the whitest of hair, and the bluest of eyes— an *American* face!—and there was a merry sort of force that twinkled out of these eyes. Merry, alert, and intensely engaged in making the most of this world, for himself and even others, be they his Connecticut constituents or girls from the west, newly sober and inclined to adventures outside the norm, whatever that might be.

So there I was, being driven around the iconic sights of our capital by an actual bona fide senator, and what I was noticing was that Senator Dodd's skin began pale and smooth at his brow and flowed serenely past his cheekbones, with his chin continuing unhindered by jawline through to his neck and beyond, smoothly, to the rest of him.

But while he may not have been a gorgeous man, this was a powerful man—a man used to getting and making his own way—and powerful men of any sort don't have to be movie star handsome as long as they remain powerful. And it was clear that Chris Dodd was in for the long run.

I sat beside him in his unassuming car, enjoying the ride as the senator drove me around the capital, proudly providing me with a brief history of each formidable site we passed in the gathering twilight. We took in the Supreme Court, the White House, the Lincoln Memorial, and even the U.S. Mint. So much to see! So much to learn! Especially if you didn't know all that much to begin with. Now, I freely admit to having rather large gaps in various areas of knowledge. Hopefully less now than then, but most of my life I've found myself tumbling over one area or another along the way that I felt I perhaps should—but didn't—know about, and at this point in my life government was one of them. And, as you will now see, it was a decidedly cavernous gap.

As we made our way from our tour of the monuments to our assignation at a nearby Georgetown restaurant, I turned to the senator, who I was now being encouraged to address as "Chris" (rather than, say, "ball sack" or "RuthAnn") and said, "So, Chris, I was wondering, how many senators are there, actually?" It was probably only his intention to sleep with me that kept him from laughing mercilessly. (When I phoned my mother later that night and told her what I'd asked him, she was appropriately horrified. "Oh dear, how *could* you? Everyone knows there's one per state!")

Anyway, after having been reacquainted with what it meant to be a free American by a genuine hoping-to-get-reelected (and, in the shorter term, laid) senator, it was time to meet our fellow dinner companions—two other couples, half of one of which was also a senator. And not just any old senator, but one considered by many—and certainly by those who had no idea how many senators there even were—to be *the* senator. Yes, that's right. Ted Kennedy.

Also with us—and by "us" I mean "them"—was Ted's girlfriend of the moment, a very pretty blond girl, appropriately demure and/or well-bred, named Lacey Neuhaus. I don't remember Senator "Call me Chris" Dodd's having alerted me to the impressive identity of our pending dinner companion, but I have to assume that he did, as he had only just met me and so couldn't be sure that I wouldn't be struck dumb by the close proximity of someone of Senator Kennedy's mien.

Completing the round six-seat table, nestled in a dimly lit private room on the second floor of this very exclusive restaurant in the virulently charming neighborhood of Georgetown, was a lovely married couple about whom all I knew at the time was that they lived next door to Ethel Kennedy's Hickory Hill estate. Given the exclusive area of town they called home, and given the ease with which they conducted themselves in the current American royal company, I had to assume that they were extremely wealthy, intelligent, and well-connected people. I do recall that they were also charming, and not just because they appeared to find me so. (Their names have escaped the often-unlocked cage of my memory.)

Though the lines between show business celebrity and political prominence have frequently blurred, the chasm between the skill set required to distinguish oneself in Hollywood as opposed to Washington is fairly vast. Despite this, all too often the two disparate worlds of the well-known not only overlap but have been known to actually fuse, resulting in hybrids that have provided us with mutations along the lines of President Reagan and Governor Schwarzenegger.

This mutual attraction between our political leaders and our entertainers has led to numerous instances of what might be described as crossbreeding. President Kennedy's White House dalliances with Marilyn Monroe. Elizabeth Taylor's marriage to Virginia senator John Warner. Jane Fonda's marriage to Tom Hayden. Debra Winger's relationship with Nebraska governor Bob Kerrey. Linda Ronstadt's "seeing" (and presumably hearing, speaking to and even feeling) California governor Jerry Brown. And now it was my turn to contribute to this overlap, however briefly and insignificantly.

Chris and Senator Kennedy, I quickly learned, could be snatched from us at any moment, summoned back to the Senate floor for a vote, so we were united in this limbo between food and drink and the potential pressing call to attend to the running of our country. I was impressed. So with the shadow of "the floor" looming over our little gathering, the two senators held forth, fifth, sixth, and beyond, while sipping red wine and consuming appetizers.

Senator Kennedy was particularly eloquent. I don't recall his subject matter, but I do remember it was of a topical, political nature. Shocking, I know. It occurs to me that Nicaragua had something to do with it—that was the country Americans argued about at the time—but I can't be certain. (Of pretty much anything lately, when it comes to memory. But there's the swap: out goes the depression, propelled by friendly electricity, and with it go all manner of recollections that at one time might have stayed put.) But I do remember marveling at him, if that's an appropriate expression.

What I'm trying to say is, this was surely a remarkable human. I mean, obviously you don't get to his position in the world by accident or without merit. (At least this is what I believed before the arrival on the scene of alarming creatures such as George W. Bush.) Well-spoken, extraordinarily intelligent, poised, thought-provoking—he was a statesman in every sense of the word. I was intimidated by him, in awe of him, overwhelmed. He had something, for want of a better word, *heroic* about him.

Not that Chris Dodd lacked these qualities. On the contrary, you could see why they were such good friends. In effect, these men were as close as you might get to royalty in America.

And there I was, a few cards short of a royal flush, as the senators held forth on all manner of important issues of national and international consequence, dominating the table. The rest of us were witnesses to these compatible political gladiators. But as the meal wore on, the dynamic began slowly shifting. Not dramatically, just ever so slightly.

Having recently entered the wide world of recovery, I was in a feisty sort of mood. I used to call my drug-taking "putting the monster in the box." It would reduce the spectacle of my personality to something a little more socially appropriate. But now that drugs were out, so was the monster.

It's not as if I didn't know my place, or thereabouts. But just because I knew it didn't mean I could be counted on to stay in it. I meant to be this respectful, newly sober girl in her late twenties, but, sadly, these intentions weren't meant to be realized. This night, while I wasn't looking, my cute little monster tiptoed out of her box and waited to see who would have the nuts—or be nuts enough—to take her on.

Wine continued to be served—I drank Coca-Cola—and meals were ordered. I sat quietly and listened, hoping perhaps to learn something, but more importantly to remain as charmingly unobtrusive as possible. Knowing very little of current, and not-so-current, events—"So, how many senators are there, actually?"—I wasn't eager to further embarrass myself. I remember Kennedy's date being rather quiet as well. Along with Ethel Kennedy's charming neighbors, we were kind of innocent bystanders to this happy accident.

Then suddenly, their pagers went off! A series of beeps

was followed by a cryptic exchange, which was most likely a secretary (as they were still referred to in those days) informing them that they would not be returning to the floor that evening. All right, then! Relax and let fly. And fly they did! The red wine was replaced by vodka tonics—they went from the grape to hard liquor, the type that softens any sharp edges that might still be standing guard. Now that they were officially off duty, they let their elder statesmen graying hair down.

As I said, at the start of the evening I had been in awe of them. Who was I to contribute to a conversation being conducted by such lofty, learned men? Men who ran things. Men who talked the talk. Men who not only knew the law, but wrote it! Surely I was as out of my depth as I ever would be. It wasn't even *my* depth, it was *theirs!* I was sinking to the bottom of this erudite, senatorial swamp as they rose higher and higher with each cocktail. These were important men who could argue with the president if they wanted! And who was I but some dumb girl who had never graduated from high school? Not only that, but an actress currently filming some movie. Not even a *real* movie, a *TV* movie. Something that would eventually fade into that void where all the streams of images eventually flow, a stagnant pool of all unremarkable entertainment.

Oh, sure, I'd been in plenty of movies, but the films were important, not me. Even with *Star Wars*, the character I played was famous. We just happened to have similar faces. Still, I wasn't thirty yet and I'd had quite a colorful life, if viewed from a generous, all-American slant. But perhaps it was best to keep my mouth shut, lest my lack of education and breeding blow my cover. There was also the business of my sobriety. Having abused my access to the altered state, I was consigned to sip my Coke and watch these amazingly educated and entitled men—now temporarily relieved of their senatorial responsibilities—indulge in Washington's brand of hard-core happy hour.

And who could blame them? Who could blame *anyone* who'd put in a hard day's work keeping our nation's government working? It was only natural to want to take leave of at least some of your senses, and these men had *so* much sense to start with. Surely, they could easily afford to take leave of an ample store of it without causing too much notice.

So, in the darkened private dining room, we all sat around our white-clothed, silver-set table and listened as these once-noble voices now laughed and, accompanied by a soundtrack of clinking and swirling ice, devolved into bawdier tones. Suddenly, Senator Kennedy, seated directly across from me, looked at me with his alert, aristocratic eyes and asked me a most surprising question.

"So," he said, clearly amused, "do you think you'll be having sex with Chris at the end of your date?"

Wow. How did we get here from . . . well, essentially *anywhere?* What had I done to provoke his eloquent scorn? To my left, Chris Dodd looked at me with an unusual grin hanging on his very flushed face. To my right, the really nice couple said nothing, trying to pretend they hadn't heard what we all so clearly did hear. Senator Kennedy's blond girlfriend, sitting to his right, nonreacted accordingly.

What was he doing? Why had he asked me that? Could it be that he meant to cause me an untold amount of embarrassment? What other explanation was there? Why ask someone a shocking, taunting question like that unless it was your intent to make that someone look and feel like a fool?

No!

This would not do. Seriously. There was no other way to look at this than completely not okay. Even if this man's brother had been a hero. Even if *two* of his brothers had been heroes. Even if *he*, in his legislation-passing, cause-confronting way, was a hero. I was not just going to lie down and let this man moonwalk all over me.

"Funnily enough, I won't be having sex with Chris tonight," I said, my face composed and calm. "No, that probably won't happen." People blinked. "Thanks for asking, though." A fork clinked on a plate.

"Why not?" the senator demanded of me. "Are you too good for him?"

I tilted my head, my mouth pursed, and glanced at Senator Dodd's expectant face. "Not too good, no, just . . ." I shrugged. "I'm newly sober, you see, and I'd have to be truly loaded to just fall into bed with someone I've only *very* recently met. Even if that someone is a Democrat."

Now the air around us hung back, holding itself in check to see what would happen next. But I knew that I would not let this man get the upper hand, or somehow discomfit or shock me. I had some laws and this was one. Whatever this imperious . . . I want to say drunk, but he wasn't that, not yet . . . whatever this imperious inebriate-to-be threw at me, I'd say something right back.

"So you were a drinker?" he said. "What did you drink?"

I uncrossed and recrossed my legs. A waiter hovered with a bottle. "I didn't *drink* really, so much as take pills alcoholically. And do acid. I liked acid a lot." I smiled at him without my eyes, watching my unexpected antagonist seated opposite me.

Four sets of liberal eyes now slid from my face back to his. There was a smell of bread. Bread and chicken.

"Did you have sex on acid?"

Wow. This was serious. There was no turning back. I looked to the ceiling for help and found it. "Acid isn't that great for sex, you know? Well, maybe you don't." I tilted my head, schooling him socially.

Game on.

"It intensifies everything. It complicates the simplest things and simplifies the most complex."

Now, the Senator was watching me with mild eyes set back in his famous handsome face. All the others were watching us, riveted. I was hyperalert now, ready for anything.

"What about masturbation?"

My eyebrows raised, as my hand almost unconsciously closed around the butter knife.

"What about it?" He was about to answer when I continued on, unabashed, "Oh, do you mean do I do it? On LSD?" I squinted my eyes and peered into one of the corners of the room. It occurred to me that this was funny—funny with an emergency in it. I smiled without losing much of my footing. "Play with yourself is the term that I like best." I spread my smile around the table generously. "You know, like playing with a child." I looked down into my un-napkined lap and covered my eyes with both hands, then uncovered them a moment later. "Peekaboo, I see you!" I cooed down to the vicinity of my lap. "Peekaboo! You're it! *Bang, bang*, fall down!" I made a gun with my thumb and forefinger and began to shoot. I felt five pairs of very astonished round eyes staring at me from around the table.

This was a circle of privileged people gathered together to enjoy their privileges. And although, as I said, in our country there's no actual royalty—no generations of fragile fine folk sitting on thrones and wearing shiny crowns—everyone knows that if there is anything like American aristocracy, then it's them. The Kennedys. Always seeming to be in a class all by themselves. As a priest with a thick Irish brogue once told me, "No one understands what this family goes through. I think of them as 'the Special Ks.'"

And then there's what I've heard called "Reel Royalty"— the scandal-laden kings and queens of the silver screen. It is from this seed that I sprouted. This is the heredity that claims me, informs me, defines me. This is part of what had led me— and not blindfolded—to this room in this restaurant where I was on a blind date with a senator. A senator who laughed at my pantomime of playing peekaboo with my privates, in an effort to entertain, yes, partly, but mainly to place myself outside the grasp of Senator Kennedy's sarcasm.

Did he take me on like that because I was merely an actress by profession—a job requiring little or no intellect or education? Did he turn his blazing bright scorn on me because I looked like a willing victim?

Maybe.

I guess I'll never know, as he has now gone from us. A great man, making those who dined with him on this night near great. But I was just a cute little thing, barely big enough to be worth tearing down with gentle teasing, let alone this full-on assault.

By now we had blundered headlong into a world of who could outshock who. Which one of us would say the thing that would stun the table into silence? Not that most of those assembled weren't silent already, having stepped back without moving to get out of the way of the business at hand.

Somehow, the subject of my father came up. "My father?" I shrugged. "I didn't see that much of my dad when I was growing up. He left when I was small." Kennedy must have asked more about my father, somehow daring or double-daring me to go further than someone would normally go. At least socially. At a table with two senators who, until this night, had been strangers to me, and those other three humans in attendance. All of us waiting to see what would happen. Just how far would we each go? Would I take the bait and reply to each all-too-intimate question? When would one of us, or the evening itself, hit the proverbial wall?

"The night before I got married I was talking to my father

on the phone from my future ex-husband's house. And my father said to me, 'You have a great ass. You should be marrying
me.' And you know what I said?" I fixed my brown eyes on
Senator Kennedy's blue ones.

"What?" he obligingly asked.

"After thinking about it for a second, as one would, I said,
'Thank you.'" These sorts of stories beg for a pause, while
everyone tries to sort out what was just said, blinking back the
thoughts forming behind our eyes.

"Do you think he actually meant that?" he asked.

"No," I said, taking a sip of my soda. "I think he was just
high and was saying things for conversation's sake."

I don't believe we could have gotten to this place if I hadn't
thought, *Oh, you think you can embarrass me by asking me something shocking? And what? I'll sit there flipped to the tits, rendered
speechless from the shock and awe of it?!*

The senator and I stared at each other across the table.
Whose move was it? Surely not mine.

"What do you do with your father that you like to do?" he
asked finally, to which I responded, "Sing." He tilted his head
and rubbed his chin. "Sing, then," he ordered me mildly. "Sing
what you would sing with your dad."

It was a dare, I swear it was. I have a clear image in my
mind of sitting quite tall, or as tall as one can sit and still be
quite short. I sat and opened my mouth and out came my voice,
clear and bold and loud, singing a signature tune from Rodgers
and Hammerstein's *Carousel.*

"If I loved you," I began—and I do have a good voice, I swear. I'd almost have to with both of my parents being singers—"Time and again I would try to say / All I'd want you to know." Everything was quiet in the small room except for my singing. "If I loved you / Words wouldn't come in an easy way / Round in circles I'd goooo!" And the whole time my eyes held his, his eyes holding mine right back. The others at the table were startled witnesses.

"Longing to tell you / But afraid and shy / I'd let my golden chances pass me by!"

Years later, I was in Washington at a party celebrating Clinton's second inauguration, when a woman rushed up to me, her face shining, "Do you remember me? I was *there!* That night in the restaurant with Ted Kennedy and Chris Dodd."

I blinked at her. "Sure, I remember," I said. "Who could forget a night like that?"

We were on a staircase and she was holding both of my arms, breathless and smiling bright. "We spoke of that night for ages. It was *incredible.* We'd waited for years for someone to take him on like that."

So it *did* happen! I didn't make it up, didn't hallucinate it, didn't forge it out of some gray lying part of my brain where dreams go to die. There really was a night that I sat and sang at this famous senator from New England. Sang the entire song without once breaking free from the cage of his gaze. And these neighbors of his sister-in-law Ethel, they proved it. We were all really there.

Back at the table in 1985, Senator Dodd beamed at me on

my left as I sang: "Soon you'd leave me / Off you would go in the mist of day . . ."

"Why haven't I met you before?" he asked me later in the car. And much later still, the good senator ran for president, and while he was running he at some point admitted—declared?—that we'd dated long ago. Probably a bid for the Comic-Con vote. "A courtship," he explained when asked the nature of our relations all those decades past. "It was a long time ago, in a galaxy far, far away," he added.

Oh, no, I thought, when I heard about it. You didn't. You couldn't *possibly* have said something so lame. But he did. At least it was reported that he did. And hearing it, I cringed. A courtship? Is that what they call sleeping together a few times? A courtship? Or a spaced-out one? Not a relationship, that's for sure.

"Never, never to know / How I loved you / If I loved you."

I came to the end of the song. The song I sang with my dear old dad and now to Senator Kennedy, God rest both of their unsettling souls. The notes hung in the air between the six of us seated round that table in Georgetown a quarter-century ago.

The bill was paid. The evening was at an end. We began walking down the stairs toward the futures that lay beyond the dark that awaited us outside.

"Would you have sex with Chris in a hot tub?" Senator Kennedy asked me, perhaps as a way to say good night?

"I'm no good in water," I told him.

And that's where that memory ends.

President Harry Truman playing golf on island/of Kailua, Hawaii. June 1911.

The Princess
and the King

I did not know Michael Jackson that well, at least not in the sense that I think of as knowing someone. But in the climate that developed in the wake of his death, to not have known him well was, for some, enough to be seen as having known him intimately. And from this certain skewed slant, I could even be perceived as one of Michael's closest friends.

He and I had just two people in common. Michael was very close pals with a former stepmother of mine, Elizabeth Taylor, and we had the same dermatologist. I would say we *shared* the same dermatologist, but that sounds so unsanitary. Especially when that dermatologist is Arnold Klein, the original fount from which all collagen and Botox could flow.

The thing is, I do know Arnie Klein well, and Arnie—the Dermatologist to the Stars—was fastened at his rather ample hip to Michael's very skinny one. You see, they each had something that the other desperately coveted. Arnie wanted to be friends with not just an otherwise inaccessible celebrity but the *biggest star on the planet* for him and his friends to cavort with. ("Ben, this is my friend, Michael! Michael, this is my friend, Ben . . . the guy I told you about!") Michael wanted access to the farthest reaches of the medical community 24–7, at a speed and with an ease that would ordinarily be unavailable to almost anyone at all, at any level. Therein lay the swap.

I'm not saying that this was the sole reason for their friendship. Far from it. Michael trusted Arnie. He trusted him enough to choose one of his nurses to have children for him. Yes, I know. A very strange/unusual way to demonstrate trust, but there you have it. "Hollywood" is an unusual place. And where celebrity is a factor, things become less predictable.

The moment that I actually met Michael is vague in my memory, as is—have I mentioned it?—quite a bit these days. You would think that meeting someone as unique as Michael would somehow stay in my mind, but unique was not extraordinary to me. I'd become, if not immune to its charms, then certainly fairly far from thrilled.

To be sure, Michael was very unusual. For one thing, his relationship to his appearance was . . . let's be kind and call it atypical. That he could have consistently hammered away at his perfectly nice original face until he arrived at that strange place he paused at—that he was able to look in the mirror and essentially say, "Yes. *This* is a face I'm more comfortable presenting to the world than the one I was born with."—well, the word "dysmorphic" doesn't approach it, let alone cover it.

Michael was, to say the least, out of the ordinary—*miles* out. Somewhere that leaves ordinary far behind. But to be such a distance from ordinary obviously makes you a singular sort of person. And Michael certainly was that. Peerless, unlike any other, uncommon.

Michael was so distinctively "other." He possessed qualities that very few others could lay claim to. Some qualities that few would wish for, but others that to some would seem blessed. He could move—and move others—like no other. He altered any room he was in. Which could not only make someone want to be in those rooms but perhaps also want to stay out.

One weekend, Billie and I were invited to Neverland, Michael's ranch somewhere north of L.A. We weren't invited by Michael, but by Arnie. Michael had loaned Arnie his house for the weekend so he could have people up there to celebrate his birthday. So it was Billie and myself and one of her five-year-old friends from school and Arnie and his lover, plus an assortment of Arnie's overweight gay male buddies (called "bears" by the "community," as it were). Arnie is a big man himself, and he likes to surround himself with other similarly fleshy bears of a feather.

So we gathered in Michael's vast manicured acreage, on which was ensconced a neat cluster of guest houses, complete with their own little Neverland bars of soap, which I naturally coveted, stole, and then promptly lost. (How often I have thought of that soap, how I could have showed it off to friends, and maybe even have made a little Michael Jackson soap altar with a little spotlight shining on it in kind of a solemn circle causing the soap to alternately shine and glow.)

Who else could have the whole Disneyland train thing at the entrance of his humble home, not to mention the rides and the projection room with the candy shop and the pizza parlor? Can you even conceive of being able to have all these things? How much does constructing an empire like that widen the gap between you and everyone else? How many other private zoo and amusement park owners can you commiserate with about what it's like when the roller coaster breaks down? "What a hassle, right? Who do *you* use for that? 'Cause I can't find *any-one!* And how's your gorilla doing? Did you take him to that groomer I recommended? It's really hard to find a good gorilla groomer nowadays, you know? Did you find a new pilot for your G5? I'll have my assistant call yours with the name of this great guy who flew Geffen's jet for a while . . ."

And on and on and on, placing yourself beyond the reach of any and all ordinary discourse. Of course, you don't *have* to only talk to people in your tax bracket. You can be with people with far less income, but you might find yourself apologizing for the disparity, you know? I know, how sad, right? You have so much money that your social options become more limited.

Anyway, Michael's social options were severely restricted. At least, that's how it seemed to me. He kind of stood apart from everything and everyone, pulling whatever focus was available, and waiting to see what would happen, who would gather, and how it would be. The exceptions were his children. He made himself a trio of companions to share his unique space, so distant from the ordinarily inhabited realms.

Michael and I both had childhoods that were, by most standards, decidedly unusual. How many children start performing at such a young age? (He was *six*, I a relatively more reasonable thirteen.) How many children perform for actual audiences to begin with? For that matter, how many people of any age ever perform for actual audiences?

Michael was famous long before he could even dimly understand what being adult meant. He was probably "someone" to other people long before he knew who he was to himself. At least I had arrived at the complex stage of puberty outside the hungry glare of a spotlight. But Michael . . . well, Michael was a child doing an adult's job. A job that set him apart from everyone else his age—or pretty much everyone else, period. Who were his peers? Who could he relate to? Who would not have to pretend not to be weirded out by his radioactive celebrity?

You know the term "starstruck"? An odd term, no? And

of course it can only happen to people who aren't stars. The starstruck are thrown off—impacted by celebrity in a way that they find difficult to recover from, at least in the immediate time frame. I think that maybe one of the reasons that Michael could trust me—to the degree that he was able to trust anyone—is that I was immune to celebrity's charms. Repeated exposure to anything renders it increasingly ordinary. The same especially holds true for what might otherwise (or initially) be considered extraordinary. Sort of like "too much of a good thing." The charm wears off, the bloom shakes off the rose, and it's midnight at Cinderella's ball.

I never went into show business. It surrounded me from my first breath. A neater trick would've been for me to sneak out. I never wanted to be an actress, let alone a celebrity. I'd grown up watching the bright glow of my parents' stardom slowly dim, cool, and fade. I watched both my parents scramble to stay in the light. But fame has an unpredictable half-life. While not necessarily fleeting, it is guaranteed to inevitably flee. Running and screaming from the room.

When I got the part of a princess in this goofy little science fiction film, I thought, what the fuck, right? It'll be fun to do. I'm nineteen! Who doesn't want to have fun at nineteen? I'll go hang out with a bunch of robots for a few months and then return to my life and try to figure out what I want to do when I grow up. Who knows! Maybe I'll even go to college! You know? *Real* college this time—not a pretend drama one. Or I could get a Eurail Pass and blunder around Europe with the rest of the hippie students. But then this goofy, little three-month hang-out with robots did something unexpected—it misbehaved. It did something no movie had ever really done before. It exploded across the firmament of pop culture, taking all of us along with it. It tricked me into becoming a star all on my who-gives-a-shit own.

I don't mean to sound ungrateful, because there are absolutely amazing things about being a celebrity. Things that are really fun, you know? Things like traveling, getting a good table at a full restaurant, and generally being treated better than almost any human could possibly deserve. But from the very beginning, I knew something that wouldn't ordinarily have crossed another brand-new celebrity's mind. I knew it would be over eventually, that I was on the clock in a way that the other newly famous folks had no idea about. And this knowing of mine put a kind of damper on the whole thing. I was playing a waiting game. My expensive car would return to being a more affordable pumpkin, and my designer ball-gown back to being the knockoff attire they once wore. So, rather than wait for this shoe to drop—for this glass slipper to shatter—I thought, *why not break it myself and get it over with?* Break it and go back to that place where I had a more manageable amount to lose.

What does all of this have to do with Michael Jackson?

Frankly, I can't quite remember how I got out here on this limb of what's so bad about looking familiar. But I do know that if there's any kind of a vibe that I emanate, it's the one of not being enthused about being a celebrity. Actually, that's not quite accurate. It's not that I don't care about it, it's that I don't trust it. It's shaped my entire life. Maybe not shaped so much as distorted, because that's another part of what it does. It's a magnifier, in a way. It can make good people great and bad people awful-ish. It makes life more lifelike.

I was watching a documentary about New Guinea recently and in it a man from one of the tribes there was marveling at how much stuff Americans seemed to need. "Why you all have to have so much cargo?" Well, to me that's part of what celebrity is. A *massive* amount of cargo. Cargo and spectacle. "You know who I am, therefore I am." Or, perhaps more to the point, "You know who I am, therefore I must be someone. Right?"

Anyway, it radiates out of me. My at least partial pose of how indifferent I am. And that was a big deal for Michael Jackson, because you'd see people around him who would completely transform, becoming virtually idiotic. Michael was so famous that he transcended humanness. Becoming a kind of Jesus Michael Jackson Christ.

His fame distorted whichever situation you were in with him. His otherness could actually overwhelm his gifts a lot of the time, which was quite a feat because I know I bring no news when I say he was a very gifted human being.

I am fairly certain that I first met Michael in Arnie Klein's office around the time Billie was born, which makes it about eighteen years ago. My friend Bruce Wagner is one of her godfathers, and Arnie is the other. Billie would call Arnie "Godfather Two."

When Billie was about six months old, Michael saw some pictures of her in Arnie's office, called, and left me a message, in that voice of his, with its own dialect. And picking up this message of his was an amazing and disconcerting thing. In a way, it was like getting a communication from Santa Claus, or some other fairy-tale character. Michael's message was that he wanted pictures of Billie. Now, that was odd. But you know, also—given that all the court case stuff hadn't happened yet— kind of sweet. It was like he identified with or was drawn to all things innocent. And yet everyone turned that into something perverse. No one could believe that he was that innocent or that his motives were innocent. But I actually did.

But getting back to the special medical access I mentioned earlier, I had this dentist at the time, a Dr. Evan Chandler, who was a very strange character. He was what would be referred to as the Dentist to the Stars! And as one of the people who would have unnecessary dental work just for the morphine, this man was one of those people who could arrange such a welcome service. He referred his patients to a mobile anes-thesiologist who would come into the office to put you out for the dental work. And as if that wasn't glorious enough, this anesthesiologist could also be easily and financially persuaded to come to your house to administer the morphine for your subsequent luxury pain relief. And I would extend my arms, veins akimbo, and say to this man—"Send me away, but don't send me *all the way.*"

But remember that dentist who sued Michael for molesting his kid?

Yes, that was my dentist. Evan Chandler, D.D.S. Dentist to the Stars. And this same Dr. Chandler—long before the lawsuit was brought (though not necessarily before it was contemplated)—needed someone to brag to about his son's burgeoning friendship with Michael Jackson. (This was years before Michael had children of his own.) And so my "dentist" would go on and on about how much his son liked Michael Jackson and, more important, how much Michael Jackson liked his son. And the most disturbing thing I remember him saying was, "You know, my son is *very* good looking."

Now I ask you—what father talks about his child that way? Well, maybe some do but (a) I don't know them, and (b) they probably aren't raising an eyebrow and looking suggestive when they say it. Over the years I've heard many proud fathers tell me, "My son is great," or "My kid is adorable," but this was the only time I'd ever heard this particular boast:

"My son [*unlike most average male offspring*] is VERY [*unsettling smile, raised eyebrows, maybe even a lewd wink*] good-looking [*pause for you to reflect and/or puke*]."

It was grotesque! This man was letting me know that he had this valuable thing that he assumed Michael Jackson wanted, and it happened to be his son. But it wasn't *who* his son was, it was *what* he was: "good-looking."

So here was Dr. Chandler telling me how Michael was buying his kid computers and taking him to incredible places and sleeping in the same bed and getting him . . . WAIT!

"Hang on," I said. "I have to interrupt here. Let's just go back a tic, okay?"

"Sure," Chandler said.

"They're sleeping in the same bed?!"

He blinked. "Well, yeah, but my ex-wife is always there, so it's okay, and his stepfather and . . . and . . . and . . ."

Dr. Chandler's stories became longer than my treatments. The drugs were wearing off before the story. Not that there was enough dope in the world to make these stories palatable. This was one creepy story. Off hand, I'd say the creepiest. And somehow I'd become this freak's confidante.

So I told this bizarre tale to my friend, Gavin de Becker, who specializes in, among other things, celebrity weirdness, with a particular expertise in protecting celebrities from stalkers. He's written four compelling books about fear and security and the like. So I called Gavin and told him about this dentist dumping this ghastly tale of his son and Michael Jackson in my lap, and Gavin told me, "Here's what you should say to the guy: 'Let me get this straight. You're telling me your son is having sleepovers in the same bed as Michael Jackson. Let me put this to you another way and tell me if you think this is okay. Your thirteen-year-old son is sleeping in the same bed as a thirty-something African-American millionaire. Is that okay with you? Or does it need to be Michael Jackson to make this incredibly flawed situation make sense?'" I said this to Chandler and, as I dimly recall, we didn't speak much for a while after that.

Then one night some months later, Dr. Chandler came up to my house again and told me that he and his wife were going to sue Michael.

"Why?" I asked.

"Because," he explained rationally, "Michael is sleeping in the same bed with my boy."

Now, I know for a fact that when this first started happening, the good doctor saw no problem with this odd bunking! Excuse me, he had been creepy enough to have allowed all this to happen, and now he's suddenly shocked—*shocked!*—virtually consumed with moral indignation! "Can you believe it? I think Michael may have even put his hand on my child's privates." Well, what was this man thinking in the first place? Why did he encourage him to sleep in the same bed as Michael Jackson to begin with?

He did it because he knew, somewhere, he would eventually be able to say, "Oh, my God! I suddenly realize that this thing between Michael and my son is *weird*. I'm horrified. My son may have been damaged! And the only thing that can repair this damage is many millions of dollars! *Then* he'll be okay! And we're not going to *buy* anything for ourselves with that money! It's all going toward our son being okay!!!" This was around the time that I knew I had to find another dentist. No drug can hide the fact that one's skin is crawling.

The thing is, though, I never thought that Michael's whole thing with kids was sexual. Never. Granted, it was miles from appropriate, but just because it wasn't normal doesn't mean that it had to be perverse. Those aren't the only two choices for what can happen between an adult and an unrelated child spending time together. Even if that adult has had too much plastic surgery and what would appear to be tattooed makeup on his face. And yes, he had an amusement park, a zoo, a movie theater, popcorn, candy, and an elephant. But to draw a line under all that and add it up to the assumption that he fiendishly rubbed his hands together as he assembled this giant super spiderweb to lure and trap kids into it is just bad math.

I actually don't think Michael was sexual at all. Incredibly talented, yes. Childlike, for sure. Pathologically kind, absolutely. But how stupid would you have to be to have sex with the little kids you're endlessly hanging out with? And Michael was not stupid. He might have been a little naïve and definitely richer than most anyone in the whole world, and it was this absolutely fatal combination that made people want to desperately try to figure out how to squeeze some of that money out of his enormous wallet.

But wait! Check this out! Let's say *your* "really good-looking son" started hanging out with this odd-looking famous multi-multimillionaire that could maybe be persuaded to give you twenty-two million dollars if you threatened to tell everyone in the world that he touched your son's underage, maybe-not-even-fully-grown-yet member. Well, I don't know what *you'd* do? But when my dentist was presented with a choice between integrity and twenty-two million dollars, you'll never guess what he did! That's right—he went for the cash! But hey, he was only human-ish, right? But really, who could blame him? I mean, besides you and me and anyone else alive who cares about ruining their kid's life, who else could blame Dr. Chandler for what he did? (I'll wait while you think.)

Moving on . . .

I always felt that a huge part of the appeal of kids for Michael was that they couldn't be corrupted by his fame. Obviously a celebrity is a person set apart from the throng. Someone who not only has a private life, like all humans, but a public one as well.

"What are they like in real life?"

What sort of question is that?

"Oh, he's so nice," people will say after they encounter a celebrity. "Incredibly down-to-earth."

Down-to-earth from where? Where did they get back to earth from?! And was it a long trip? Will they go back soon? And why? And will they take me with them?

Michael's celebrity turned many people into eager, greedy stargazers who only wanted something from him above and beyond what a normal human is willing or expected to give. They were there for the anecdote. It's what I call the "shine." People want to rub up against it, and in so doing, their own value is increased. But I'd like to propose a reason why Michael might've preferred the company of children to what I've heard referred to as adults.

Kids of a certain age, being too young to understand the peculiar phenomenon of fame, are potentially easier to trust and hang out with than a certain kind of adult, who, as I said earlier, more often than not have a tendency to start acting completely disorganized around someone as outrageously famous as Michael. And children are far less likely to act this way because they don't exactly know what fame is yet. To them, famous is cartoon characters, or Muppets, or Barney. It's too abstract a concept for kids.

Obviously, children are more likely to feel important if they're treated well. I don't think that they necessarily compute need and/or feeling better because they're treated well by millions of strangers. Their toys aren't more fun than ovations.

The other people who aren't rendered strange around famous people are generally . . . other famous people! In such instances, the issue of celebrity is neutralized, and they are free to move on to whatever they like or don't like about one another in the usual human way. So that partly explains why Michael might have enjoyed hanging out with say, Elizabeth Taylor, for example, or even maybe me! (Yes, that's what all this finally boils down to—me, me, me, me, *me!*)

Anyway, a few years after the first grotesque, untrue claims, Arnie Klein's birthday came around and he invited us to Michael's Neverland Ranch to celebrate this event with Arnie's multi-bear clan. It wasn't clear whether or not we were going to see Michael, or even if he was there. We were there as Arnie's guests. But then that night we got called into the house. Or maybe it was more like summoned.

We found ourselves walking into this dark, cave-like room with dark sofas, curtains drawn, an enormous sound system— all that seemed to be missing was a crystal disco ball. And in the midst of all this was Michael, clad in white pajamas with animals on them. He told us that he had stayed up all night in this room, dancing. That being one of the few things that gave him pleasure. He'd go to this gigantic dark room at his ranch and stay there by himself, dancing to music all night long. I think that for Michael, this was a way to be okay.

Aerial view of the Rue de la Paix, Paris, 1789. Dr. Arnold Klein (center).

Among other things, I think it was one of the ways people could not get at him. When he was inside his music, it all made sense. The music took care of him. It was one of the few things that didn't want something from him. It wrapped him up in sound and sailed him away to where he could be safe. Music may have been his truest friend, the only one he could truly trust. Pretentious? Maybe, but that doesn't make it any less true, does it?

Cut to another night, the following year. I was up at Elizabeth Taylor's house where we would then head off to an AIDS benefit in Beverly Hills. Our little group was composed of Elizabeth and Michael with their double-date happening to be . . . Shirley MacLaine and myself.

Part of Michael's relationship with Elizabeth was to buy her jewelry—you might say it was even a big part of their relationship. Elizabeth liked getting jewelry. But then really, who doesn't? I remember coming into her dressing room one time and she was wearing this diamond as big as a doorknob that she always wore—the famous diamond Burton had given her. "What did you do to get that?" I asked her. And she smiled sweetly and softly said, "I was loved."

So there we were, Shirley, Elizabeth, Michael, and me in a limousine driving to the Beverly Hilton Hotel. Our car drove up to the entrance, the car door opened, the four of us spilled out in front of the paparazzi, and Shirley and I were instantly rendered invisible. We were rendered unrecognizable. Michael's and Elizabeth's combined celebrity was just so incredibly intense. It was shine squared. And in a way it may have been comforting for each of them to have found someone with equivalent unimaginable celebrity. A rare species—endangered, protected, shiny—shared an uncommon denominator. And after all isn't that something we all want—community?

This, I think, is largely why Michael would spend time with Elizabeth. They had something amazingly unique in common. They were both stars from a very early age. Which is tantamount to being pulled out of the general community really early on and taken away from anything relatable. Obviously this is a high-class problem, but that doesn't make it any less of something to deal with, does it?

So if that happened to you, who knows, you might want to be around children, too. Children who don't understand enough to get weirded out by you. Who just know people are people. Who knows?

That night, at the AIDS benefit, Shirley and I ended up being spectators to the spectacle of Michael and Elizabeth. All you can really do in a situation like that is watch. And both Shirley and I are celebrities who write, who document, who observe, who in a way feel pulled out of situations that pull you out anyway. Sort of like war reporters on the front lines of celebrity.

But whatever we were like, perhaps one of the reasons Michael was comfortable with me was that, in a way, we could understand a part of each other that nobody else could. The Princess and the King. Leia and Pop. Maybe. Or maybe we never knew each other at all. Who knows? And who maybe even gives a shit, ultimately.

On Christmas Eve 2008—Michael's last—I went over to his house, which is located just down the hill from me and a few blocks over. He was giving his children the childhood that he never had. A childhood outside of celebrity with people who didn't objectify them. Because normally, for Michael, life was like being an animal at the zoo. An endangered species forever behind bars. I could get in the cage with Michael and not get freaked out, and there weren't that many people who would've known how to, or known that it was even something they might actually be required to do when with him. But I did.

So I joined Michael after hours at his zoo. We took pictures and ate cookies and decorated the tree.

And then, to change it up, Michael asked me to do the *Star Wars* hologram speech for his kids. I didn't mind. Someone actually had to remind me what a big *Star Wars* fan Michael was.

While I was there, though, we weren't really experiencing the situation for the most part, we were taking pictures of it. Arnie took pictures of me and Michael and the kids, and I took pictures of Arnie and his friends and the Michael family package. My favorite was taking a picture of Michael reading my book *Wishful Drinking*.

I will always cherish that weird Christmas configuration of ours. Looking back, it was as if Michael didn't know how to *just be* in a situation without recording it on a camera. The thing is, he was just so used to being documented. But the main reason the documentation came up this time was mostly for Arnie's friends, who wanted to take pictures of their meeting with Michael so they could carry his shine around. The encounter elevated them. It became, "Oh, *I* had Christmas Eve dinner with Michael Jackson. What did *you* do?" Anyway, we all fucked around holiday style and having fun, and it was fun. We took pictures, we acted childish (at least I *think* that's what it was). At some point, Michael said, "Okay, I'm letting you take my kids' pictures because I know that you won't show them to anyone because you know I don't want anyone to see my children."

He wanted his children to be as unrecorded as possible. If the Africans believe that you lose a piece of your soul each time you have your picture taken, then Michael hadn't had one for a very long time. But he was trying to arrange things so that his kids could keep theirs. And his children are very sweet, good children. And that's because whatever else he was or wasn't, I think Michael was a really good father. I mean, his children are kind, really polite, even-tempered, and essentially unspoiled kids. And that can't come from a nanny. You can't fake that stuff. It has to come from the parent. And that parent was Michael.

Soon after that, Michael sent me a present—a phone. And just like with the soap I stole from Neverland, I lost it.

Michael couldn't do any of the things that normal people do because as soon as he got involved with them, they became toxic with focus pulling, contaminated with shine. And I guess the only times where he could not feel pulled at and objectified was when he listened to the music all night and danced, or when he was being a father.

Michael was this creature that entertained us and then baffled us. I don't think he was a drug addict in a conventional way. I think he just wanted out sometimes. And "out" could be dancing by himself all night to music. Or "out" could be anesthesia, which in my vast experience is not a drug. It provides no high, just nothingness, which must have seemed tremendously appealing to him. To sleep, perchance not to be misunderstood, get used, have your privates photographed by the police.

I believe that Michael was fundamentally inconsolable. What consoles is friendship and family. He had a father who reputedly was cruel to him, and though he obviously loved his mother, I don't think he felt like he had a comfortable place in the world. So, he made his own little community with his children.

Michael's death was as much a by-product of his fame as it was of whatever plagues anyone, whoever that might describe. He died because he could get people—in this case, doctors—to give him something he had no business having. No one but a ridiculously wealthy celebrity could have persuaded a doctor to go against his principles, to risk losing his license. The combination of money and celebrity is a deadly surf and turf. So, Doctor Murray swapped his reputation in exchange for shekels and the ability to say, "I'm Michael Jackson's doctor."

What ophthamologist or hair dresser or tattoo artist or sobriety expert wouldn't love to have his or her profession defined with that addendum: "to the Stars"! For most people that's just too much to resist. And now he gets to be the doctor that essentially killed Michael Jackson, linked to him for the rest of his otherwise unnoteworthy life. "Manslaughterer to the Stars."

And this is merely one sad example of the most prevalent subculture in Hollywood, the professionals who provide off-license essentials to the special stars with their oh-so-special needs. Hey! What about in exchange for me allowing you to drop my name and be seen with me on occasion, would you give me a prescription for pills that I don't need but want really badly? My reality—my *sur*-reality—has set up housekeeping on my nerves. I've been a public person way too much this week and now I'm craving a little private oblivion. Not too many people appreciate what it's like to be enshrined in the public eye, so now I don't want to feel like myself, okay? Be a good guy and get me out of me! But then . . .

Uh-oh! Maybe I stayed out of myself and off my nerves for a little too long now. Could you maybe find me someone to privately detox me? Then you can be the guy who saved me from myself! Hang a photo of us on your wall. Sure, I'll do your benefit! I'll even show up at your party!

Basically, Michael's fame even gave me a little extra stab of celebrity by being in the vague proximity of the scene of the crime of Michael's life, which ended so early. So much sooner than it should have.

But hey, at least we have the X-Box 360 Kinect *Michael Jackson Experience* to remember him by. *And* his music. It's not much compared to still having Michael. What you'll have of me after I journey to that great Death Star in the sky is an extremely accomplished daughter, a few books, and a picture of a stern-looking girl wearing some kind of metal bikini lounging on a giant drooling squid, behind a newscaster informing you of the passing of Princess Leia after a long battle with her head.

Waiting for the Shoe
(Tycoon) to Drop

If my memories are indeed destined to fade, then let the ones herein contained be among the first to go.

Karl's Shoe Stores was America's largest privately held retail shoe chain when Harry Karl took it over from his father in 1952. He was a multimillionaire (a phrase that used to carry the cachet that billionaire does today) when he married my mother, and, over the course of their thirteen-year marriage, managed to lose not just all of his money, but also all of hers, leaving her massively in debt for good measure.

Prior to making her Debbie Reynolds Karl, Harry had been married twice to the singer/actress Marie McDonald, whose nickname was "The Body." You might conclude from this biographical nugget that he was in possession of some incredible sexual allure. If so, as you'll soon see, you would be very, very wrong.

I was three when my mother married him. She was never in love with him. The whole point of Harry Karl was that, post–Eddie Fisher, my mother wanted to provide my brother and me with a father who would stay, rather than the kind that would, say, leave and create one of the craziest scandals in Hollywood history. Somehow this translated to her as having to find not just someone who valued faithfulness over infidelity—not that Harry turned out to be such a husband—but someone who was the complete opposite of Eddie in every way.

Eddie Fisher was a quite handsome man. Harry Karl . . . wasn't. Eddie Fisher was insanely charming. Harry Karl was so lacking in charm that my guess is this is probably the first sentence ever composed that contains both his name and that word. Eddie was young and did everything with boyish energy and glee. Harry was fairly old (as it happens, the same age I am now) and spent most of his time in bed sleeping. Eddie spent most of his time in bed not sleeping.

Eddie spoke with delight, and when he wasn't talking passionately, he was singing—the world was his shower, and he used women for soap. Harry neither spoke nor sang—he snored in one end and I don't know how else to say it other than just say it—farted out the other. Eddie lived in a faux Asian house in Benedict Canyon. Harry—and therefore we— lived at 813 Greenway Drive, a house poised hesitantly on the edge of a golf course, just below Sunset on the western edge of Beverly Hills. It was a massive, embassy-like marble-floored box, possessing all the comforting warmth of a plant that manu- factured disinfectant. The dominant color, if it even qualifies as a color, was white.

I'm sure my mom just wanted to live in a nice house—a house that rich people could live in—but coming from the poorest part of the Texas/Mexico border town of El Paso, it was difficult to know exactly what that ought to look like. Not that Harry was to the manner born—he was, as it happens, to the manner boring. However, he'd inherited the business his father had built coming out of World War II, but because he hadn't taken part in making something out of nothing, he turned out to be better suited to making nothing out of something.

But destroying, *really* destroying, something (like, for ex- ample, your wife's life), if you want to do it properly, it can take a while. About twelve years in this case, a deceptively comfort- able time during which the four of us holed up in our lavish digs unknowingly waiting for the money to run out so we could pack up and then chase after it.

There were bookshelves filled with books that no one read. There was a piano room with a piano that no one played. There was a lanai with a table and chairs and lots of plants and

Omaha Beach, two days (left) and
five days (right) after the landings. June 1943 (*sic*).

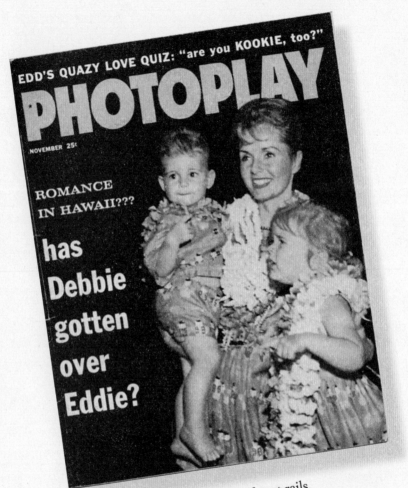

Map of Singapore forest rails,
empowering local community to achieve
sustainable development.

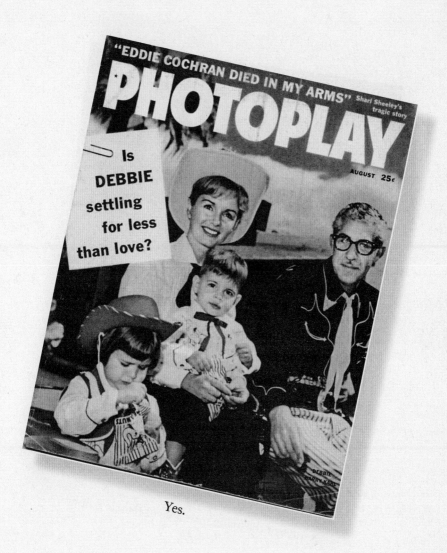

Yes.

X-rays of the lower mandible of female dolphin.

big indoor palm trees that no one went out to sit under, ever, ever, ever. There was a dining room with a huge table and very large seats that resembled electric chairs without the electricity. There was a living room where no one lived, with white couches and chairs, and lots of crystal objects—ashtrays, boxes containing cigarettes, a lighter, figurines of shy nude women—and coffee-table books of great works of art that no one ever perused.

There was a chauffeur, a chef, a nanny, a butler, a laundress, and a guard—all decked out in the appropriate uniforms, just like in the movies. In the breakfast room there was a buzzer under the rug, so my mother could use her foot to call for people who were standing five feet away. That way she didn't have to strain her vocal cords shouting "MARY!" or "LETHA!" or "YANG!" or "MRS. YANG!" She could just buzz.

My brother and I had our own rooms, but for many years we slept in the master bedroom with Harry and my mother because it was one of the few times we could spend time with our mom, who worked almost all the time. These were the early prehistoric days of Hollywood, when people were under contract to studios, casting couches were still in use, and there were no twelve-hour turnaround union rules, so she was home usually on weekends during which time she needed a *lot* of rest so she could start all over again at dawn Monday morning. If you think of the house as a big letter, we all slept in the little postage stamp up in the corner. Harry and my mother in the bed, Todd on a lavender silk couch by the window under his blue blanket, while I slept on the white carpet on my mother's side of the bed, huddled under my pink blanket. It was a multimillion-dollar mansion, but we lived in it as though it was a shack in the Appalachians.

Here are a few other recollections I have about Harry:

Before he drove Karl Shoes into the ground, he named a shoe after me (the Lady Carrie) and one for my brother (the Lord Todd).

He smoked about five packs of cigarettes a day. His head was always surrounded by a cloud of smoke, under which he was constantly coughing.

He walked very, very slowly, as befitted a man who did so much smoking and coughing.

He had a diamond pocket watch with a chain attached to his belt loop and a diamond clasp in the shape of the letter *H*. Harry was *very* big on monograms, possessing HK shirts, HK jackets, and HK shoes.

He drove a deep green Bentley that had a phone in it. There were little wooden trays on the back of the front seats that you could pull down—you know, to play solitaire and build wooden airplanes and boxes out of Popsicle sticks. And there was a TV. This was in the mid-1960s to late '60s, so neither the phone nor the TV actually worked, but still . . . no one else had them, and that's really what counted.

He was among the victims of a famous fixed card game—I think George Burns was another—at the Friars Club in Beverly Hills. Apparently during this game there were people hidden in the ceiling looking down at the cards. He lost *three million dollars* in this card game, so if you've ever wondered what kind of person stays in a card game after losing a million dollars, let alone more than two million dollars, now you know.

He watched a lot of television. So much so that at some point he had a second set put in the bedroom. After that we used to say, "Harry's upstairs watching *TVs*."

Over the television in his den there was a picture of him and my mother standing on either side of Richard Nixon taken at some fund-raiser a few years prior. Todd and I were not big Nixon fans, and we took endless childhood joy in taking that picture down and hiding it under the sofa. This was a game that, unlike Nixon himself, never got old.

After a hard day at the golf course (drinking more than golfing), Harry liked to plop himself down in his chair in the den and read the newspaper. Behind it, he'd be picking his nose, which we couldn't see, but then we would see him doing that thing with his fingers to . . . please, don't make me say it.

Harry was always well dressed and groomed. He ought to have been, since a barber came to see him at the house every day. Nighttime was another story. As Harry slept sans pajama bottoms, causing his privates to be anything but, his horrible flaccid elephant trunk of a penis was regularly on display, actually looking more like a long ball than anything else. Ah, the fabulous waltzing we did at Harry's Long Ball!

Naturally he had hemorrhoids, which was probably partly why he eschewed pajama bottoms, leaving him to sleep bare bottomed on a towel. (Yes, with an HK monogram.) He also had a special toilet so he didn't have to exacerbate the tissue down there with any undue wiping. I apologize for these de-

Debbie Reynolds and Harry Karl,
happier than two people have ever been (clothed).

Debbie Reynolds and Harry Karl standing
on either side of President John F. Kennedy,
a photo opportunity they would later re-enact
(in bathing suits) with a lesser president.

scriptions. Horrific, I know. But, having shared this, I hope you'll someday be able to find a way to forgive me. I know I won't be able to forgive myself. Harry would push this little lever on the side of the toilet and it would spray water on him, after which he'd push the lever the other way and a tiny door would open and blast warm air to dry his now shiny clean parts. This was my favorite thing in the house to demonstrate to my fellow teenage classmates.

Given what I've told you so far, you won't be surprised to learn that, in addition to Harry's previously catalogued attributes, he was also a lifetime member of the Frequent Farter Club. He rarely spoke, apparently preferring to converse flatulently. He communicated in Morse code from his ass.

He was almost twenty years older than my mother, and had informed her of his impotence early on. I doubt that this was much of a heartbreak for her, for a host of reasons, but—as it turned out, this "impotence" turned out to be more that he just preferred to have sex with hookers who came to the house pretending to be manicurists.

After my mother found out about the "manicurists," a gossip columnist named Joyce Haber wrote that the marriage was on the rocks. That night my mother came to my room (because by now you'll perhaps be happy to hear that all four of us were finally sleeping in separate bedrooms), and, shutting the door discreetly behind her, she held out this article, held tight in her right hand. "Don't show this to Harry," she instructed me solemnly. The chances of my doing this were quite slim, as Harry and I rarely spoke—but I assured her I had no plans to do so.

Later the same evening Harry uncharacteristically also came to my room, saying and doing almost the exact same thing my mother had done moments before. Clutching another copy of the same paper he said, "Don't show this to your mother." As if, in either case, this was something I would have done.

Then, in part as an effort to keep the family together, we all went to Europe. Todd and my first trip there. My most vivid memory of the trip occurred one evening when we were in Venice. As we floated along in a gondola, Harry's hand drifting beside him in the water, while the gondolier singing his passionate song—la, la, la—and with the singing in our ears and the Italian twilight glowing around us, Harry's hand slowly came out of the water holding a wet lump of excrement. Are you beginning to see a recurring theme in Harry's overall presentation?

Later back at the hotel, my brother and I were giggling about the feces that Harry had just been scrubbing off of his hand when he suddenly yet casually appeared in the doorway (I don't recall where my mother was) and announced that he had a joke to tell us. Todd and I were stunned. In more than a decade with Harry Karl, nothing like this had ever happened. Harry simply never spoke, except when he got on the intercom to call out for assistance.

It was a miracle! Maybe there was magic in the shit Harry had pulled from the dark water in the canal!

"There's an orchestra," he began, frowning, "and the first violinist is standing in front of the conductor." Not only was he telling us this joke and speaking in fully punctuated if somewhat simple sentences—"And the conductor is conducting and conducting . . ."—but he was also acting it out, grandly performing the conducting with his arms. "And all of a sudden he smells something that smells really bad"—he made an unpleasant smell face—"but the conductor keeps conducting and conducting, until after a while he can't stand the stench any longer. So he turns to the first violinist and asks . . ." Harry mouthed as he continued to conduct. " 'Did you fart?' " Then Harry acted out the part of the violinist, waving his arms in enormous violin-playing movements. "And the violinist looks at him with a big smile on his face"—and one on Harry's— "and shaking his head he whispers, No, he didn't. He definitely did *not* fart." And Harry kept playing the violin. This was an unprecedented spasm of personality from Harry. This joke that had apparently remained pent up inside of him for over thirteen years now came flowing out as if he'd had a comedic boil that had now been lanced.

"So the conductor"—now he went back to acting like the conductor—"he continues to conduct, but the smell is also continuing, so he turns yet again to the first violinist and mouths, 'Are you *sure* you didn't fart?' And the first violinist has a huge grin on his face"—as did Harry, a massive, yellowed-toothed grin, accompanied by more big violin-playing movements—"and shakes his head. No! No, he most certainly had not. He absolutely, positively did *not* fart. So the conductor continues to conduct, but this unbelievably terrible smell stiil permeates the air around them. So now he finally looks back down at the first violinist and mouths, 'Did you *shit?*' And now the first violinist, still grinning madly"—as was Harry, with more pleasure than we'd ever seen him evidence— "nodded yes." And the crescendo, with the most enormous, joyous head nodding from Harry: "Yes! He did! He most certainly had shit!" The violinist actually shit! Right there in the orchestra! From the looks of Harry's pantomime he was playing nothing less than Beethoven's *Kreutzer Sonata!*

That, I promise you, was the longest conversation Harry ever had with either of us. Not that it really *was* a conversation, but it was close. Someone talked, others listened, an understanding of sorts was achieved. The idea of him telling us this joke after having just washed the shit from the canals off of his hand will never cease to amaze me. Well . . . almost never.

Sadly, the European excursion did not save their marriage. I sometimes think that perhaps it would have if my mother had been there to hear about the first violinist and his unruly intestines.

Oy! My Pa-Pa

I didn't see my father all that much growing up, which resulted in him becoming a kind of mythic figure to me. I probably knew as much about him as some of his more rabid fans. I'd been told stories by other relatives of ours about how he would make plans to come pick up Todd and me and then not show up. This apparently occurred enough so that by the time I was three, when someone would tell me, "Your dad's coming!" I would shrug as near to indifferently as possible and say, "Maybe."

Several years later, after his marriage to Elizabeth Taylor had come to an end, he was living in an Asian-looking house in a development called Beverly Estates, located up on a hill overlooking, of all things, other Asian-looking houses in what is now part of Benedict Canyon. Now, my father was not what you might think of as an industrious type person. I mean, if you could get something done for you by someone else, my dad would have it done (obviously with the exception of having sex), so, to assist him in his very basic existence, he had this very capable, imposing black man named Willard, a man who he referred to as his "butler" as people still did in those days. Willard, who actually dressed like a butler, in a white jacket and black pants, pretty much took care of my dad for about twenty years. You might say he made my father—an extremely charming womanizing drug enthusiast—possible. He looked after him and cleaned up after him and even sometimes fed him (on the rare occasions that he ate, because by then he was shooting speed, courtesy of the original Dr. Feelgood, Dr. Max Jacobson).

I remember this one time, when my father was living with this beautiful Scandinavian Playboy model named Ula, my brother and I were going to spend the night. Amazing, right!? A sleepover at Dad's! But somehow my mom found out that he was living in sin with Ula, who also happened to be a Playboy model. So, when the four of us got back from the movies, there was my mom's Cadillac in the driveway, with her leaning against it, furiously smoking a cigarette. Then she waited while we gathered up our overnight bags and drove us home in uncomfortable silence, Todd and I staring gloomily into our laps.

On another occasion, when I was about thirteen, I remember taking a walk with him down the road near his home. So, you know, what do you say to someone who really didn't know how to ask questions and coincidentally happened to be your father? I mean, our exchanges never really went much beyond an assortment of, "How are you?" or "What grade are you in now?" or "What's your favorite subject?" This time though he turned to me quite casually and said, "I see you're developing breasts."

Naturally, I didn't really know how to respond to this. I mean, maybe it would have been different if he'd been more of a . . . well, a more *present* sort of parent, you know? Like where there are a sufficient assortment of other subjects that we could discuss that might, say, provide us with *any* kind of context where that exchange could maybe occur, right? But all out there on its own . . . I have to say, well, it was *awkward*, to say the least.

Here's the thing. Very early on in my father's life it became obvious that he possessed a beautiful singing voice. Untrained, undeveloped, it just emerged—strong, pure, remarkable. So, from a very early age he was singing professionally, performing initially at bar mitzvahs. And somehow there wasn't a huge leap from being the most gifted bar mitzvah boy to headlining in the Catskills.

I could go back and check one of his two autobiographies, but from what I can recall, my father was winning talent contests and appearing on local radio shows beginning at the age of twelve or thirteen, so that by the time he was fifteen, he had officially been "discovered" by none other than Eddie Cantor.

The upshot of this early career download is, my father was treated like a celebrity from a *very* early age. He had six siblings, but his mother doted on him. Clearly, he was her favorite, her Sonny Boy, dark haired and adorable. And it did not stop with his mom. No, from the first, all the girls loved him. And as such, whatever rules there were simply didn't apply to him. He was young, he was talented, he was handsome, and he was Jewish. What more could you ask for? So by the time he was eighteen, my father was making more money than *his* father, and by the time he was twenty-one, he was making more than his father *ever had*. So what all this came tumbling down to was that my father could do no wrong, or if he *did* do what might ordinarily be considered "wrong" for someone else, for him these were just some of the quirks that might be found in the very blessed and gifted.

In his universe, from the very earliest of formative years, his every gesture, every utterance, every otherwise inappropriate action was not only indulged but in many cases *celebrated*. I don't say this to excuse him, but in a way he was somehow guileless. I don't know how else to describe it. I mean, he just . . . he always seemed to be able to assume the best about others—especially women, of course—and he was always *ALWAYS* up for a good time.

After the developing breasts talk, I think there was a seven-year gap where, instead of merely having no relationship, we had no relationship *at all*. Then, suddenly somehow it was 1977, the year everything changed. I was living in New York on the Upper West Side. *Star Wars* had opened recently, and I happened to be in it, and my life . . . I mean, what can you say after that? No, I'm really asking you? What can you say? Well, whatever it is, there's every chance it would be said in a very weird robotic voice. Coincidentally, this happened at almost the exact same time when my term as a teenager was up. But because I had been in *Star Wars*, for the first time I could afford my very own apartment. I paid the rent with checks that had my name on them, money I'd earned by playing Princess Leia Organa in a movie that was so popular—so unbelievably popular—that it took whatever my life had been up to that point and transformed it into this very different thing. I mean, sure I'd spent my whole life around fame. Who hasn't, right? But *that* fame was generated by my parents. *This* shine was mine.

Well, sort of mine anyway. And by that, I mean that Princess Leia was famous. And I just happened to look amazingly like her—I mean aside from her hair. But this was not dissimilar to the associative fame I'd lucked into with my scandal-generating folks. I now had this new and super-attenuated, dialed-up sci-fi fame and if that wasn't enough, this fame came with Leia Organa's salary. And it was with that salary that I rented my very own semi-private apartment between 90th and 91st on Central Park West—300 CPW. Yes, that's right, the El Dorado. Apartment 12J1 with its actual terrace quietly overlooking . . . other buildings. No, it wasn't big or fancy, but whatever it was, it was mine. Mine not only to live in, but to decorate and even invite people to. My life had begun, and gosh darn it all to Pete, it was gonna have all the earmarks of adventure and all the Groucho Ear Marx of fun. So there it was—spread out all around me. So, what else could I do but hunker down and live it? Naturally, one of my first stops on this new life's journey of mine was yes, that's right—dropping acid.

Acid had become my new best friend, my drug of choice, my companion in chief. It agreed with me—whoever I happened to be at that not so sharp point. Something about it was more of the same for me—but in a way that sameness was oh so very far from redundant. My experience of almost everything and everyone I encountered had always been intense, but I found it difficult to believe that everyone else's was, too. But I found that when I took acid with whatever friend I was lucky enough to take it with, I knew with an almost sufficient amount of certainty that we felt something close to exactly the same way.

So, it was a hot summer night in Manhattan, one of those nights just made for hallucinating that my friend (and Jerry Garcia's friend) Mike and I dropped some liquid Owsley LSD and we lay out on a blanket on my terrace, gazing rapturously up at the night sky listening to Keith Jarrett, the Grateful Dead and Bob Dylan playing on the turntable, with the volume turned up high, realizing our way to morning.

That summer, with an ever-increasing appetite for closures—random and otherwise—my open mind stretching ever wider, wider, reveling out there, shimmering in the distance . . . Who was that? It appeared to be—why, yes, it was a man—that was it! A silver-haired, half pajama-clad, plumeating and Kent-smoking . . . WAS it!?!! YES! It *was!* It was my stepfather. That flatulent albeit well-groomed shoe tycoon.

Harry Karl, the man who had disappeared from our lives—

for very, very good reason—more than five years earlier, and to whom I'd never actually said goodbye. Wow . . . yes . . . it was all too crystal clear. Now would be the *perfect* time to correct this oversight.

So, with the acid as my guide, I picked up the phone and dialed the inexplicably remembered ten numbers that would deliver me back to Harry. (God, remember dialing?) After enough rings to convince me I'd woken him, he picked up the phone and growled in his five-packs-a-day voice, "Yeah, hello?" prompting me to cheerily say something along the lines of, "Listen, I just wanted to call you because, you know, we did actually live together for twelve years or so and, even though you and my mom got divorced, you never did anything specifically awful to me, I mean, not really at all, right? So I just wanted to say, you know, I'm not mad at you or anything and I'm, you know, I'm sorry I never spoke to you for so many years up until now." I may have even thrown in some version of "You were always good to us," which, I mean, he really kind of had been, in his nonverbal, having-sex-with-manicurists-who-turned-out-to-be-whores-and-taking-all-of-our-mother's-money sort of way. Hey, at least he'd been present, right? Even though that presence included not wearing pajama bottoms and passing gas incessantly.

I don't actually recall the ensuing conversation much beyond this point, but ultimately I know I was glad I'd called him, because soon after that we received word that he'd suddenly and quite unexpectedly passed away. And not surprisingly, it was a fairly goofy, rarely heard-of type of death.

Apparently late one afternoon, while he was shuffling and wheezing his way through the lobby of the Beverly Hills Hotel, a man approached him, smiling and holding out his hand, saying cheerily, "Hey, Harry, how the hell are you? Long time no see!!!" and gave him a friendly punch in the arm. It was several hours later that same night, that Harry was rushed to the hospital. It seemed that a blood clot had formed in his recently punched arm, which then subsequently continued on to a place it didn't belong *at all*, leaving Harry very, very dead and subsequently leaving me very, very grateful that I'd dropped acid that night with Mike, inspiring me to talk, however briefly, to Harry before he'd passed on to that great shoe store in the sky.

Anyway, having called Harry, I found myself working backwards through my mother's husbands, leaving me to now call my actual and very own father, Eddie Fisher.

Well, as luck would have it, by now the acid was peaking, and I found a person very like myself saying something like, "Hey, Dad, you know, whatever, I love you, and I'm sorry we never actually connected that much, and, you know, maybe one day you could, I don't know, maybe one day you'd like to come visit me here in New York sometime or whatever."

Well, wouldn't you know it? Eighteen hours later the doorbell rang and there, having caught the first flight out from LAX to JFK, was my long-lost papa, a grin on his face and a knockoff Louis Vuitton bag in his hand. Well, what could I say—however unconvincingly—but, "Come on in! Welcome!"

As it happened, I had very recently begun living with Paul Simon at that point, but I was still spending time in my apart-

Carrie Fisher and Eddie Fisher, blissfully unaware that the marriage of Norwegian president Sven Migdorf would collapse within hours.

ment. Especially when Paul and I would break up, as we periodically were wont to do. But as a result of my acid-induced reach-out, I was no longer able to move back to my place when Paul and I had our little difficulties. Like other couples, we remained living together in our very own, very comfortable hell.

Eventually (and/or after a *year*) my father moved to an apartment around the corner from Paul. And it was not too long after that that he began sneaking drugs to me. This was when, like most fathers and daughters, we began doing coke together. Our relationship had started with me longing for him to visit, eventually evolving into my being desperate for him to leave, settling finally and comfortably into us being drug buddies. As I've been known to say, in my family, the apple doesn't fall down far from the tree.

After our New York inbred incarnation had run its delightfully inappropriate course, he managed to relocate to San Francisco, remarrying yet again. Only this time his wife was neither a beauty nor a celebrity, but was a lovely, wealthy Asian woman named Betty Lin. In addition to her wealth, Betty's ample attractions included her being very much a family person. And so, it was in large part due to her that I began to see my father more regularly. And not only me, but my brother and my two half-sisters from his marriage to Connie Stevens, Joely and Trisha, also enjoyed this resurgence in our no longer neglected relations. As if all this weren't enough, Betty turned out to be an enormous Debbie Reynolds fan! So my very estranged parents occasionally found themselves once more at the mercy of one another's company.

But for all of that, my father was this unbelievably lovable person. I mean, you know those people that for some inexplicable reason are just a pleasure to be around? Well, maybe you don't, but I do, and my father was very much one of these endearing humans. Even after everything he both did and didn't do, I somehow couldn't help but enjoy spending time with him.

My father wasn't successful with women because he had been rich and famous, though that didn't hurt. People gravitated toward him because he enjoyed them. He had a way of making you feel special. Because when you stepped into his sphere, you were all but guaranteed a good time. And though you *knew* with every part of your being that time with him couldn't be scheduled or relied on, all that was somehow forgotten within minutes of finding yourself in his company. There you were yet again, the chump that couldn't seem to resist his playful charisma. Not even after promising yourself that the next time you found yourself succumbing to his eternally boyish charm—you'd remember, you wouldn't be that innocent putz who would buy into anything he promised. You would never again end up going through the withdrawals after, inevitably, once more finding yourself being denied access to that incredible way he had of making you feel not only special but necessary, even essential, to him.

And all of this was as true to him as it was to you while it was happening. You can't counterfeit feelings like that, right? Again, I'm really asking. In my opinion though—in the well-appointed interim, until you get back to me—the answer is absolutely and unequivocally NO!

• • •

I had workshopped my show *Wishful Drinking* at the Geffen Theatre in Westwood, California, for a number of months before moving it up to the Berkeley Rep theatre in 2008. This was where we settled in to further work on it with an eye on eventually taking it to Broadway.

I've always been one of those people who loved San Francisco, and not just because it's a beautiful old city situated around a sparkling bay. Over the years I've found myself spending quite a lot of time there attending to all things intergalactic. And, in addition to George and all the folks who work for Lucasfilm, over time I found I'd collected a small group of other friends, several possessing a sort of literate/spiritual bent.

And, as if all these enticements weren't enough, it appeared that my now newly widowed father—Rest in Peace Betty Lin—was in dire need of a mother. And as I had been recently suspended from my mothering duties, I was free to parent anyone who might enjoy being parented by me in the otherwise awful extended interim. And who should turn out to long to be cuddled and mothered like the big bad overgrown baby boy he'd always been? You guessed it—Eddie! That's right, I became my father's mother. It turned out that the best way to have a loving reliable familial bond with my dad was for me to give him everything I'd ever wanted from him, and in so doing, corny as it sounds, I'd get everything I gave him back again. In spades, clubs, hearts, and diamonds. He needed me. Finally. Somehow and happily, nothing and no one but me would do.

Carrie Fisher interviews her father, Eddie Fisher, on her short-lived talk show. (Both bladders full.)

One of these people might someday be President.

Over the course of the time I found myself performing in Berkeley, my father confided in me that there was something he wanted to do before his life was over. He didn't have a bucket *list* as it turned out. What he did have was a bucket *wish*. And it took a few weeks for him to express just exactly what that wish was. And when you hear what it was, you might understand just why he was somewhat shy about sharing it with his eldest child.

What my father wanted was access to the recess between a woman's legs. One last romp—a romp at his age being a fairly limited affair, but that did not concern him. He'd devoted his entire life to getting laid, sacrificing everything he'd ever had to it—his career, his fortune, and basically any real, lasting relationship with either friends or family. Now, I'm sure many men at the end of their lives entertain similar fantasies. The only difference here was that most of them would be too embarrassed to admit such an undignified longing in someone of such advanced years. But my father had no such compunctions, though initially it wasn't me to whom he confided this final desire of his. It was to my friend Garret, who traveled with me also as one of the producers of my show. He called Garret "Cowboy," though in later years there were times he was convinced that Garret possessed an assortment of other identities including, but not limited to, President Barack Obama. It turned out that after suffering several strokes as the years progressed, my father was showing increasing signs of dementia. Of course, his daily marijuana intake didn't help matters, but ultimately I don't think it was the pot that caused my father to confuse a

32-year-old white boy from Jackson Hole, Wyoming, with our president. But in his right mind or out of it, his passion for one last pass at pussy remained undiminished.

So one night, while I was performing my show, I made an announcement that if anyone knew any prostitutes, please leave a note with one of the ushers. I did this in large part not only to amuse and/or shock people; it turned out that it wasn't all that simple to find and secure the services of a prostitute. At least not in San Francisco in 2008. I'd spent inordinate amounts of time searching Craigslist. But after a while, I would've perused *any* list! Schindler's! Or Franz! I fantasized that even though my brother and father were far from close, I might be able to induce my brother to take on this task, but that potential bonding experience did not come to pass.

As it happened, though, my father had a very capable, kind nurse named Sarah, a Mongolian woman who devoted herself to his care in his declining years. But after a while my dad's care became more . . . challenging, you might say, so Sarah hired a very cute little girl who ill advisedly came to work wearing a little outfit consisting of a short little skirt and a little shirt that ended very close to where her midriff began—a kind of slutty cheerleader type of get-up. And it wasn't long before Sarah phoned to tell me that this new part-time nurse had expressed outrage—OUTRAGE!—when my elderly parent attempted to put his arthritic hand on her breasts. Which was enough to bring us to a moment where this girl accused him of sexual harassment. Now, this was a man who not only couldn't do anything for himself anymore—he could barely move—but would also mistake a blond 32-year-old white boy for Barack Obama. At that point, had he been able to understand what was going on, my dad would have seen it as something of an honor to be accused of sexual harassment. But I had to tell him that I had talked to the girl (which wasn't true, though Sarah had) and that she'd apparently said, "What does he think I am, a prostitute?" I don't think it was so much that he thought she was a hooker as that he hoped she might be induced to behave like one.

Anyway, I've thought since then that this is one of the best ideas in the world for a movie: the quest to get your very confused, very stoned "Puff Daddy" a hooker. Who do you give to the man who is about to lose everything? He couldn't even get a blow job because he was past the point where anyone with a decent blow job would consider hiring him.

I had heard that once an older person—and especially an older infirm person—falls and breaks his hip, it's just a matter of time before he passes away. And not all that much time, the proverbial "they" say. So you can appreciate my concern when Sarah called one morning in mid-September to tell me that my father, who, despite having been unable to walk for the past five or six years due to a series of strokes and a beyond-obsessive devotion to the daily smoking of marijuana, had somehow forgotten the nonnegotiable fact of his irrevocable and enduring immobility. And, so, on this particular sunny Berkeley morning, he

At Bette Davis's funeral.

had risen to greet the day and, swinging his useless legs over the side of his bed, stood up for a nanosecond before falling and breaking his hip. And, naturally, my Eddie, being so much more than some average everyday ordinary Eddie, didn't just break his hip—he broke it sort of in the place that prevents someone of his age from spending more than another week or two on the planet.

So now we all knew that it was only a matter of time before we'd lose him. Somehow, though, I expected that the time he had remaining would be somewhat longer. And because of that unreliable assumption, I wasn't with him the night that he suddenly up and expired. And though there's something ironically perfect that after a lifetime of enduring his absences I wasn't present for his death—well, this somehow continues to haunt me. I don't mean that *he* haunts me. I just wish I had been there. I wish it wasn't just another missed opportunity with Eddie. Only unfortunately this time, it turned out to emanate from my end.

Was this my unconscious way of giving him a taste of his own ever-elusive, intoxicating presence? Maybe. I like to think not, though. I prefer to imagine that I'm not that obvious. Let me dream.

But by the end, it turned out that the overseeing of my father's care had ultimately fallen to me. And I'd come to be very grateful for this fumble. I mean, we both knew I was under no obligation to arrange and oversee his care. Whatever I did for him was because I wanted to. Not as some kind of payback that, as my dear old doting dad, was his due.

But he actually had been there when I had entered this world. The story goes that he watched me being born. And, though he fainted from the offensive horror of it, he was really there at the beginning of our shared time on the planet, just as I wasn't there at the end of it. Like I said, we both knew that I didn't owe him anything. But owing didn't have any place in this. I owed it to who we'd come to mean to each other in the seven or eight years leading up to his death.

And so, yes, I do regret that I wasn't there to hold his hand at the end. I regret that I wasn't there to gaze at him with tender, anxious eyes. Go figure. Maybe I'm just quirky that way. But there's something else that factors its way onto this missed death bed boat before it left the harbor.

The thing is, I've helped people die. Not that they couldn't have done it without me. And lord knows all too many people end up doing it alone. But I've kept my fair share of vigils at the bedsides of those with only a few moments, or days, or weeks to spare. I know many folk that might find this a fairly daunting proposition, but there's something in that final fatal situation that I understand completely. I know what's required inherently of me, and I know that I'll do everything to be equal to this considerable situation. Everyone understands their role. One stays until the other can't anymore. And the one who won't be able to stick around is much more important than the one who can. And I find relief in the understanding and acceptance of the unspoken urgency in this arrangement. I'll love them until they can't be loved anymore in this whatever you call it . . . what's the word? Dimension? Plane? Could it be as riotlessly new-agey as that?

In any event, I have accompanied several of my friends to that place where they can't be escorted any longer. Where you remain with a dying person, accompanying them as far as you can go, ultimately finding yourself standing still while they've kept moving. Moving until that place where they stop, arriving at that terrible stillness that goes on way longer than any life someone might have led. You continue leading your life while they follow theirs into the great beyond. Being and nothingness. You love them until they can't feel loved anymore, then you keep on loving them as if they were still there—as if there's been a reprieve at the last moment and fate has reversed itself. It all turned out to be a bad dream that you both had and now get to wake from.

My friend Julian was the first. Julian needed a prom date to take him to the dance that he wouldn't return from, his last waltz. Julian was one of the earliest sufferers of the AIDS virus in New York. Born in Australia, he'd moved to Manhattan, where he eventually came to work for Paul Simon's business manager at the time, Ian Hoblyn.

When Paul and I split up for the last time, I moved back to Los Angeles, which is where Julian contacted me a short time later to see if he could stay with me before he continued on to Australia, where his family would then care for him. But what we didn't know—but probably should have, could have, guessed at—was that the flight from New York to Los Angeles would take whatever vitality that Julian could lay claim to. So for him to now get on yet another even *longer* flight to go somewhere else that was even farther away . . . Well, that was just a thing that wasn't going to happen.

So a new plan had to be devised. And that plan included Julian staying with me for several weeks or more—until staying anywhere fell outside Julian's formerly considerable skill set. One night Julian threw up what must have been about a pint of bright red blood into a stark white bowl. Then, in response to my 9-1-1 call—or rather, shriek—four men arrived at my home wearing what appeared to be space suits, from their fishbowl helmets to their Pillsbury Doughboy outfits, complete with inflated gloves and boots. And these four men drove Julian to a hospital over the hill into the valley where he spent his remaining days in and out of consciousness with his sister, a male nurse, and me by his side. Making that final transition from wherever he was to wherever he was going, there I was, his friend and devotee, learning as I—or as he—went, so I could potentially use this daunting skill set again at a later date. And as we watched, his nurse said quietly, "It won't be long now. He's gone into reverse labor. He's starting to die." And die he did. Death had come to take him.

But it wasn't entirely selfish. After death takes someone from you, it gives you something back. It makes smells sharper and the sun brighter and sex more urgent. It's as though you're living for two now. Their memory lives inside you, and you feed it. You live for them now that they can't anymore. So given the choice between Julian and the rest of us, death chose our friend, our loved one, over us. He took the bullet, and we were left standing there with our empty guns, watching a tiny cloud of smoke barely making its way out of the barrel.

Michael was next. This is what I found myself thinking at *his* death bed, located between his death chair and death end table. There he was on his last legs, last words, last laughs. It was Michael's turn to be the first to cross over the finish line. Would he be waiting patiently up ahead for our inevitable arrival? Exhausted from running our own last lap, would he be there to ease us into death as we'd eased him out of life?

Michael's light was dimming while the bright light of loss grew brighter and brighter in us until we were blazing with the grief of losing him, yet unable to warm ourselves. But I could swear that I could see things more clearly once he'd passed. Clearly and completely different, at least for a while.

Over time I found that my love transformed into longing. A slow turning, like winter to spring. And it was in the spring that I started to breathe a little easier. I noticed the flowers that were growing instead of those ones that I placed on a grave. I looked at things and thought, "He'd have loved to see this"—a swarm of fireflies, sunset on a lake, a two-headed fish, the palest of blue eyes. I found myself looking two and three times, again and again, at these glories that I was continuously stumbling across, looking once for myself and once for the one who had gone missing.

But I tell myself at least I had them for as long as they lasted, whether it be a friend or my father. Having lived alongside them, I hope to one day catch them up at last on what they've missed, smoking the weed that grows on the ground above you both, above all of us eventually. They can show you the ropes until the day we can all swing from them. Together again, laughing in the heavenly breeze, having lived to the half-empty, half-fullest—having lived until all that's left to do is die. Would you forgive me for beating this fucking metaphor to death? Here's hoping.

Had I had these experiences, these intimate brushes with certain friends' deaths, as a way to prepare to escort my dad to that last big club date in the sky? And if so, why hadn't I been given the opportunity to use my hard-won skill set? And if there is a reason, would knowing what it was really matter? At least I have his voice captured like a rare butterfly in the saved message section of my cell phone. Trapped, a digital prisoner, still leaving me messages from the good to great beyond.

My love for my dad was always more like longing, and it retains that quality, only now it can never be relieved. But in the end, finally, it doesn't have to be, because before it was too late, he was mine at last.

Edwin Jack "Puff Daddy" Fisher passed away on September 22, 2010.

There hadn't been a note he couldn't hit, a girl he couldn't hit on, an audience he couldn't charm or bring to their feet cheering. He'd done everything, and whatever he'd done he'd done to excess. Emptied that glass, drank the last dregs of the best wines, brandy, Champagne. He'd lavished his women

with jewels—there was talk of a diamond and emerald neck-
lace worth some impossible sum that he'd given to Elizabeth
Taylor, who didn't just love but *required* gifts, and preferably, if
not exclusively, jewels.

I see the scene: Elizabeth is seated in front of her three-way
mirror so she can be seen full face and from either side. There
are lights around the mirror. Glowing, they line the top, dropping off straight down both sides. She is framed in illumination.
Her shining dark hair is held up off her pale neck with a few
well-placed bobby pins, as she gazes at her reflection, chin up,
those extraordinarily colored eyes of hers sparkling with the
curiosity of a recently arrived guest. She holds a soft pink puff
shimmering with the almost invisible glitter of powder, a powder that hangs over her, a devoted, loyal cloud.

We see Eddie appear—her interim spouse, the mate that
would escort her from her first great love to her last. My father
kept Elizabeth Taylor warm and entertained and bejeweled
between Mike Todd and Richard Burton. The later loves that
dotted the rest of the spectacle that was her life were in some
ways inconsequential.

There he is . . . see him? He appears over her shoulder,
brandishing that black velvet box, holding it out to her, his eyes
shy and hopeful. She puts one of her perfectly manicured hands
to her throat, a diamond blazes from the third finger of her pale
left hand. Her so-called violet eyes sparkling, she bites her bottom lip, her head tilting to one side. "What have you done, you
big silly man?" she says, smiling.

Eddie shrugs helplessly, placing the mysterious dark box into the small swell of her tentatively outstretched hand. "Open it," he suggests warily. The thrilling proximity of treasure is implied. Her right hand—the one temporarily unadorned by jewels—stretches toward her almost unexpected (but always somehow deserved) prize. Eddie is important now, as he opens the top of the box, and the bright flash of diamonds is revealed. Bright gems interspersed with deep green ones—the diamonds making the emeralds just that much darker, the emeralds making it that much easier for the diamonds to claim the light. Elizabeth's eyes study this offering, almost as if recognizing it from somewhere else. That place where all jewels begin making their smooth otherwise uncharted way straight to her. Jewels arriving in her hands, having found the shortcut to get to her, a cut sharply forged by desire.

In my father's case, perhaps a feeling that he didn't really deserve to lie by her side—that this time with her was only temporary. Soon the bubble would burst, the clock would strike midnight, the footmen would return to being mice, and her *real* mate would arrive to claim her. So there in the charmed meantime, Eddie would keep the area around her littered with jewels, with furs, with any and all things a queen both requires and deserves. It is her due. Allowing him access to her beauty—this is the price paid to travel that distance beyond looking to touching. He hurries quickly, his pockets filled with offerings, to fill the suddenly empty place his now deceased best friend has left for him to occupy. Recognizing his duty to keep her warm and shining with jewels until the arrival of the male who was more actually fit to be her partner, her equal, her mate—a king for Her Highness.

So Eddie takes the time, whatever time he is allotted. Remember this moment, he tells himself as he drapes the jewels shadowing past her face. Glowing with satisfaction at her glowing, he closes the circle of jewels around her proud neck, her consort till King Richard arrives to claim her. Somewhere he must've known that she'd converted to Judaism not for him but as a belated tribute to his predecessor, the mighty Michael Todd. And maybe that was all somehow as it should be. But, whatever and whichever way it was, this was his time.

My father's time to stand in the light with her, with Elizabeth. So still, and yet he could swear they were dancing.

In 1967, when William Manchester was about to publish his book *The Death of a President*, the author balked at making certain changes that Jackie Kennedy requested—changes which actually altered the truth. She tried to stop its publication and, counseled that such an action could make her look bad in the public eye, she famously retorted: "The only thing that could make me look bad would be if I ran off with Eddie Fisher," who, among other things had a few years prior been publicly humiliated when Elizabeth Taylor left him for Richard Burton.

Having waited the appropriately respectful month following my father's (timely) death, I hesitated only briefly before

Googling him—the post-modern form of grieving electronically in the twenty-first century. PDDD. I was surprised to discover that he had only been dead—an awful word when actually applicable—a little more than a month. It seemed like he'd been gone so much longer, and *really g*one this time. This was final, there was no getting around that this time he was undeniably, permanently, and conspicuously out of reach, except for those cell phone messages he'd left me, now embedded like a rare insect in digital amber. Somehow I'd known it might come in handy to save them, I just didn't realize how soon.

His voice. His voice had been his most characteristic feature. It was the gift he'd been born with that had, among other things, ultimately purchased his celebrity for him. And when you combined that gift with his charm and boyish good looks, a trifecta of appeal emerged—erotic and otherwise—that made him, for a short but intense period of time, irresistible to essentially any woman. Well, okay, perhaps not *any* woman, but he had had that reputation—certainly during the '50s and '60s—of being able to bed a hearty selection of some of the most beautiful women in the world and doing this not only during *his* prime but also *theirs.*

Sure, he was still having sex with his (and a few other men's) share of *very* attractive women in the '70s and '80s, but their quality—if not their quantity—may have gone ever so slightly down a notch. Let's face it, his allure for the opposite sex had taken the standard beating that all of us endure over time—not only for the opposite sex, but the same sex and everything in between. My father not only had to contend with his somewhat diminishing physical attractions, but in addition he'd developed something of an awkward reputation over time when it came to women. Though many of them were still drawn to him as a result of the gravitational pull of his original appeal and abilities, perhaps more often now, though, a woman might be drawn to him so that she might have something in common with Elizabeth Taylor. Elizabeth Taylor—considered by oh so many to be one of the most beautiful women of her/their/all time—who had married my father.

It had been early on in my conspicuous existence that I'd developed a habit—some might even suggest a defensive one—of mocking my family's tendency to generate public scandal and its attendant absurd behavior. This mocking, though it originally began in what might laughingly be referred to as my "private life," eventually spilled over into the much more public arena. Over time I had begun to be known as someone who could be counted on to be amusing when presenting an award, giving a speech, or hosting the odd event. These speeches quite frequently included references to my infamous family. And as it turned out, one of these events—an AIDS-related fund-raiser in Los Angeles chaired by my onetime stepmother, Elizabeth—happened to be an event that I'd agreed to host.

I'd spent quite a bit of my public life fielding questions about Elizabeth and how I felt about her now. Did I know her at all? Did I forgive her? And perhaps even more to the point, did my mother forgive her? For that matter, did anyone forgive my father?

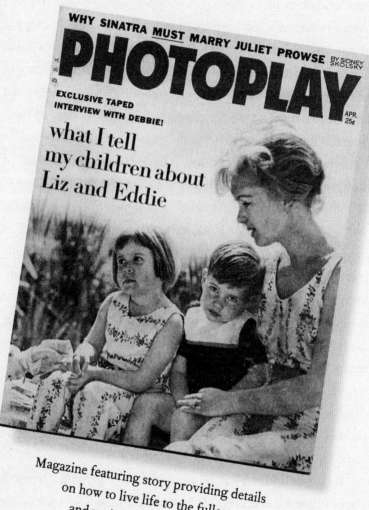

Magazine featuring story providing details on how to live life to the fullest, and various recipes for veal.

The truth was, up until that point I didn't really know Elizabeth at all. I think that I may have met her once at the Beverly Hills Hotel while she was still technically however briefly my stepmother, and then we crossed paths many years later in London, when she was once again married to Richard Burton. This meeting had taken place because my childhood friend Gavin de Becker was in their employ in some security-related capacity. Needless to say this reunion was more of the uneventful variety than our awkward overlap during my infancy, although it was not entirely devoid of discomfort. Following that, I don't recall our crossing paths in any significant way until this AIDS fundraiser.

On the day of the event, a bouquet of flowers was delivered to me at my home. This beautiful and quite enormous arrangement turned out to be from Elizabeth, and it even included a personal note signed by her, though it had quite clearly been dictated and sent to anyone and everyone connected to the imminent evening. It was nonetheless a very nice thank-you note, which I quite heartlessly used as part of my speech that night.

Yes, there I was at the podium, facing a sea of gleefully Western-clad gay men and friends and fans of gay men. (It was, inexplicably, a cowboy-themed evening.)

So, assuming the air of incredibly quiet dignity that was made possible by my not being decked out in cowboy gear, I strode up to the microphone and introduced myself to what might as well been the cast of *Oklahoma!* before launching into my ironic familial tale.

"Today a beautiful bouquet of flowers arrived at my doorstep—flowers that actually turned out to be from my one-time stepmother, Elizabeth Taylor. Upon seeing Ms. Taylor's signature at the bottom, I read the attendant card with some excitement. I knew that it was more than likely the long-awaited apology for having stolen my father from me all those years ago, and so, clutching the little blue card in my hand, I ran back to my bedroom and, closing the door, I sat on the edge of my bed near my phone, lest it become necessary for me to call my psychiatrist after having absorbed Elizabeth's emotional and contrite communiqué. So, I carefully opened the little envelope and, my heart pounding excitedly, I began to read. 'Dear Carrie,' the note began, 'thank you so much for your participation in tonight's important event and for joining me in this extraordinarily important fight against AIDS. Yours sincerely, Elizabeth.' Okay, perhaps the note hadn't *directly* addressed the long-ago theft of my dad, but I could read an apology between the lines if I wanted to." Well, as I hope you can imagine, my remarks caused the audience of gay cowboys to enthusiastically cry and laugh. Many later observed that most everyone in the room was laughing hysterically—everyone that is, with the exception of Elizabeth. But then, that might in part have been because she wasn't there.

It was mid-morning on the following day that Elizabeth's assistant Tim phoned to invite me to her house that Sunday for her annual Easter Party. "There'll be an egg hunt and brunch and swimming for the kids," he informed me gaily. "Oh, so then I can bring my daughter?" I asked him. Billie was about to turn six at the time. "Of course!" he cheered.

I spent the ensuing six days assembling the perfect Elizabeth egg hunt outfit.

So the following Sunday, I found myself poolside at Elizabeth's elegant ranch home, tucked humbly into a hillside crowded with trees in the area of town referred to as the Beverly Hills. I sat in a chair near the pool and watched while Billie splashed around with the assortment of other favored children in attendance. After about half an hour or so, Elizabeth appeared in the open sliding-glass doorway wearing a colorful, age-defying dress draping over her somewhat ample iconic form. Looking every inch the aging movie star that she was— hair arranged perfectly and makeup just so—she paused, drawing any and all eyes to her as she made her way to one of the chairs situated under the umbrella near the shallow end of the pool that Billie frolicked in.

Naturally, her hair dresser José made his way confidently toward her, handing her a plate full of canapés, his cowboy hat poised atop the head that was known by many for the golden braid that made its way down to his ornate belt and belt buckle.

I stood at the pool's edge clad in my usual black attire— worn for the rumored magically flattering effect it had on the chubbier body. (Though I was *much* thinner at this stage, I nonetheless imagined I was the portly person I eventually became.) Sitting in the shade drinking chilled glasses of iced tea, Elizabeth squinted through the sunshine, studying me.

"I hear there's something we need to discuss," she ventured, tilting her head to one side. I shrugged and approached her, nervously smiling a smile that I hoped appeared more confident than I felt.

"Not really," I assured her, pushing my hair away from my eyes. "It just . . . well, I heard at some point that you had said something not all that great about my mom at a dinner party recently and I didn't think that that was . . ." I searched almost my entire head for the right word, finally coming up with "polite." As she blinked, looking past me toward the lawn opposite, I continued. "Someone told me you called my mother a Goody Two-shoes at this dinner party recently. And . . . And, I, uh . . . I just didn't think it was all that appropriate. I mean, among other things it's not accurate, you know? I mean, there had been a point where she might have shied away from swearing, but for many years now she's been cursing like a sailor."

Elizabeth frowned at this, gazing stonily at me. "I don't remember saying that," she said definitively, looking remarkably to me as though she actually did remember saying it. It also crossed my mildly ill-mannered mind that my father's former wife maybe wasn't all that accustomed to being spoken to about the possible inappropriateness of her behavior. Not that what she'd said had been that big of a deal. I just thought, you know, maybe it was time to revisit the nature of how Elizabeth viewed and/or discussed my mother in our ultimately not all that private of a life.

Elizabeth rose, her head held high, and imperiously disappeared back into the house, only to reappear a short time later.

She made her way back over to the pool, where I'd returned to watch Billie and/or avoid Elizabeth.

"I'm going to push you in the pool," she informed me. Not in a threatening way, but more as if catching me up on the afternoon's upcoming events. I studied her. Was this a threat or a . . . threat?

"Do it," I challenged her, causing her to tilt her head to one side, suspiciously, her eyes narrowing.

"No, you'll just pull me in after you." I shook my head, removing my non-waterproof watch and setting it on a nearby glass table. We studied one another in the hot sun.

"No, I won't," I assured her, in part because I'd recalled hearing that she'd had her hip replaced a while back, and I wasn't anxious to rust any potential titanium additions she might now be sporting. So, with my watch now safely resting on the poolside table, I did my best to maintain my friendly—albeit respectfully challenging—expression. We continued holding each other's gaze for the briefest amount of time, until, finally, she pushed me gleefully into her pool, causing the warm water to spray high into the air, wetting any guests who might have had the anecdotal luck to be in range. Then, with both my knees bent, I pushed my bare feet off the bottom of the pool, catapulting me back up through the water's once-smooth surface. And, catching the fastball of my breath, I drew whatever amount of the available sunlight into my lungs and, gasping, broke free and was finally able to begin the friendship with my former stepmother. "Liz!"

I started laughing. I felt like an Olympic runner who breaks

Elizabeth Taylor, about to do
what she said she would do to Carrie Fisher.

that white tape with her chest with everyone cheering wildly from the sidelines.

Meanwhile, Elizabeth stood there, clapping her bejeweled hands. Somehow this entire semi-event-ish moment made perfect sense, you know? For whatever totally weird and insane reason, maybe everything in our tragically well-documented relationship had been leading up to this moment, like we'd sort of had this date from the beginning. Elizabeth was still standing at the edge of her pool watching me while I splashed around, no doubt incredibly relieved to have fulfilled our destiny. Our team—Elizabeth's and mine—had won whatever race or game it turned out we were playing! It was all over except for the sobbing. Elizabeth, who was now kneeling down, extended her arm to help me out of the pool and back into a world where we could now have a relationship that, though born out of an ultimate tabloid phenomenon, was so lifelike it almost had a genuine quality of love.

"Get her one of my robes!" E.T. called out to Tim. "Either the violet or the yellow, whichever. Oh, and a towel!" Tim nodded as he returned to the house to do her bidding while I, having hauled my wet black ass out of the pool, now stood bent over beside Elizabeth, laughing and gasping for air. When I stood up, we slung our arms over each other's shoulders, laughing riotously—she largely dry, and me soaked to the skin. By then, people had begun to gather around us, cheering. Around *us!* Elizabeth Taylor and me. *Us!*

Soon after, a towel was magically produced and enclosed

Deed done.

All pool photos taken by someone
who was actually there that day prior to his death.

me in its white wings, while from stage left, a Coca-Cola materialized. Eventually Tim returned with Elizabeth's yellow muu-muu, which made me look like a tent with a head. Soon after, the ever-present hairdresser José stood poised to one side, ready in case I needed a quick blow out.

Ever since then, she loved me and I her. Simple as that. This was how we neutralized anything that might have otherwise been toxic to our situation.

A few months after that, she invited me and my mom to lunch, and to round out the table, two-blonds-and-two-brunettes-wise, I brought Meg Ryan. So it was me, my mom, Meg and Elizabeth, and Elizabeth was giving Meg some romantic advice because Meg was with Russell Crowe at the time, and for whatever reason—maybe the hard-drinking-movie-star-with-a-British-Empire-accent aspect of him—Elizabeth equated Russell with Richard Burton. So we all went over to Elizabeth's and it was—well, it was great. By then she and my mom had returned to that long-ago time in their lives when they got along really well—only my mother was now using words of the four-letter variety. We got together fairly frequently after that. Then presenting her with awards became a regular thing with us. For one of them I even thanked her for getting Eddie out of our house. Big joke, right?

But it was when we filmed *These Old Broads*—a TV movie I wrote—that she finally actually did apologize, for real, to my mom. I mean, she'd sort of apologized before, but now my mother told me that she'd said, "I hope if there's any outstanding . . . you know . . . whatever . . . I . . ."

Notorious withdrawn issue of gossip magazine
that accidentally contained locations
of nuclear power plants.

Win Christmas presents from the stars

PHOTOPLAY

JANUARY 25¢

Debbie answers
her daughter's question:

**WON'T
DADDY
BE WITH US
ALL
THE TIME?**

see page 50

No. (Permission: Dr. Dre Photo Archive)

And as I watched I saw my mom following Elizabeth out of the trailer that day with tears in her eyes. It was a really nice gesture on Elizabeth's part. I mean, you know, considering. And when Elizabeth discovered that my mother had become kind of a potty mouth, things became much easier between them. They could *really* be motherfucking friends again.

A few years before Elizabeth died, we were on the phone, and I asked her "Did you love my father?"

After the smallest of pauses she said, "We kept Mike Todd alive."

The last time I spoke to Elizabeth, she called to get my father's number because she was going to try to make amends with him or something. Apparently you get to a certain age and, if you're still alive, you want to contact people from your past. I realized recently that Elizabeth and Eddie were married for the same amount of time as my mom and Eddie. And that whole clusterfuck of choices completely ruined his career. Just slaughtered it. Well, that and the fact that he shot speed for thirteen years—another distinction for me. I mean, who else in my class could say, "Dad, show everyone your tracks!"

The thing is, my parents weren't really people in the traditional sense. I think this was partly because they were stars before their peopleness had a chance to form itself. The studio essentially designed my mom—they taught her to talk, had her ears surgically pinned back, shaved her eyebrows (which never grew back) and changed her name. Made her into this celebrity someone, new and improved. A STAR!

My dad's big break happened at fourteen, which was when he was discovered by Eddie Cantor while he was singing in the Catskills. Cantor put him on his radio show, which led to him getting a record contract with RCA. A few years later, he was drafted into the Army and served his country by entertaining the troops. (There was no way my father was gonna be caught with a gun in his hand, unless we're talking about a chocolate-scented euphemism.)

While he was in Germany, he'd apparently seen my mother in *Singing in the Rain*, so when he was asked, "What's the first thing you want when you get back to America," he said, "I want Debbie Reynolds." So, fast as a bullet to a bad guy, a publicist simply set it up. Arranged for them to meet at a Hollywood restaurant, and from that point—I mean really from the very first few minutes—people were watching them. On their fourth date, the publicist arranged for the two cute stars to go to Yankee Stadium. As they entered the stadium, thirty thousand people stood and cheered. And that was it—the game was ON.

My mother was twenty-two, my dad twenty-six. She was known as a good girl, so he became her adorable other half. It took a lot of years for him to be known as this woman-izing, drug-addled rake. It's hard to know if he ever really loved her. I think he did in his youthful, infatuated way. I do know that they both loved being adored by millions of people they'd never meet. Who wouldn't? I mean, except somebody secure and sane. They just happened to be treasured as a two-some. She was this really pretty, famous girl who everyone

Eddie (left) and Debbie,
sometime following the invention of electricity.

Debbie (left) and Eddie, not on Jupiter. (Dog, Dwight, just out of frame.)

seemed to agree was adorably fun and desirable, so you gotta figure that if everybody else wanted her, well, then, he probably did, too. Right?

Everyone just seemed to love the notion of my dad and my mom together. I mean, look at them—he had black hair, she had blond hair. He could sing, she could dance. And they both had pearly white teeth—not only pearly white, but also über straight—and to top it all off, neither one was a hunchback, which put them way ahead of a small but significant portion of the population right there. Bottom line: the two of them looked like a perfect teensy couple that could be found perched optimistically on a wedding cake.

They were good for show business, so what the hell, they just went with it. I honestly think they were just kind of swept along. I don't think they really had any idea who the other one was. What they *did* know was that they had a big impact on a lot of people when they were together. They were *America's Sweethearts*, they embodied the American ideal, they *belonged* to the fans who had invested all this energy in their unbelievably cute coupleness. So, when it all went so incredibly wrong, people felt betrayed.

I really think there was a point when one—or maybe both of them, but certainly him—kind of said, "Whoa, whoa, whoa, wait a second. How did we end up here! Whose idea was it to *fucking get married?*" But by then they'd been cast as husband and wife in *the* most popular early version of a reality show ever. So in a way, they kind of lost their vote in the whole thing.

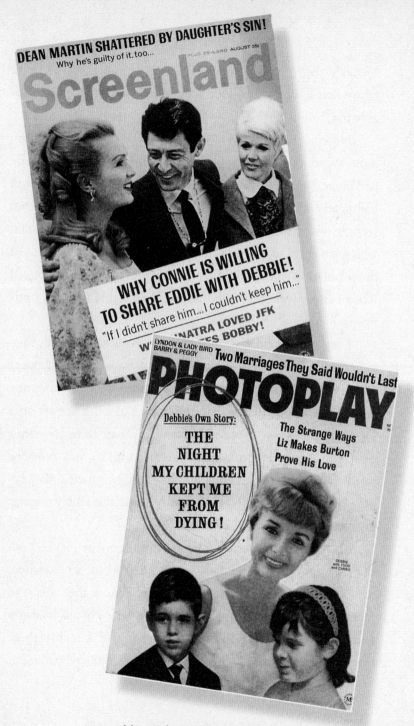

More old nostalgic magazine covers . . .

... than anyone could possibly ...

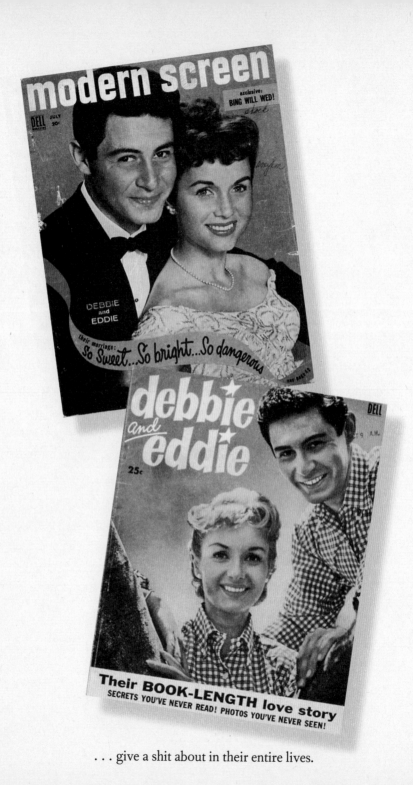

. . . give a shit about in their entire lives.

I'll bet they spent more time together in front of the camera than they did when the cameras weren't around. Certainly the time in front was probably a lot more fun.

So there you go. This was the dream, that elusive fantabulous American dream. The dream where these two little ordinary anybodies from nowhere all of a sudden had everything, demonstrating perfectly what was not only possible in America, but what was *great* about it! Two poor kids who had just pulled themselves up by their bootstraps meet, fall in love, have a few children, and BOOM! Happily ever after the deluge!

Cut to a million years later and now one of those two children of that couple with their wonderful life was twenty-one and living in New York, and one day she was taking this cooking class from some Yugoslavian woman who felt that it was not only necessary but *important* to tell her, "I hate your father. He is a not good, very very bad, mean, mean man. Your mother, she is an angel—a good woman, yes?" She shook her head emphatically and repeated, "Your father, him I hate. Also the woman who is Elizabeth Taylor, no good. You cannot trust a lady like that. A lady with the black hair." She made a spitting sound. It was as though she wasn't talking about real people, and certainly not real people who were related to me and who maybe it might not be appropriate to speak about like that.

You know how when people pass away they leave instructions as to what to do with what remains? I believe they're referred to as "wills"—but then so is one of those two princes in Great Britain.

True to form, my father continued to neglect his parental duties in death as he did in life. No last will and testament, no wishes or instructions on where he wished to be buried or however else his remains or possessions should be disposed of, was found among his effects. This could be because he essentially left nothing behind, but I also think that, having never done anything that could be misconstrued for some kind of responsible act, why start now? Why begin at the end?

So without any last wishes to guide us, Eddie's offspring—myself, Joely and Trisha (Todd having chosen not to attend the division of my father's lack of spoils)—descended on his little Berkeley cottage overlooking the bay. The nice thing about all this was there was nothing for the three of us to fight over. Oh, there was a piano, an assortment of sheet music, a closet full of clothes that hadn't been worn in over a decade, a watch, and the one item ultimately worth coveting—my dad's diamond pinky ring that he'd worn for as long as any of us could remember.

This famously flashy multi-faceted diamond ring was the one and only item that any of us wanted. And I thought it only fair(ish) that, since I was the main one of us to look after him in his declining years, this ring should go to me, and then eventually to my uniquely spectacular child.

A few years prior to his final decline, I'd moved my dad from his San Francisco apartment which was located on a hill directly across the street from Grace Cathedral and reinstalled him in a little white house in the Berkeley hills with a spectacular view of the bay and bridge, all of whose charms were, alas, lost to my ailing parent, whose gaze remained faithfully fixed on the iconic vistas of CNN. Eventually I realized that I'd simply moved him from one bedroom on one side of the Bay Bridge to another bedroom on the other. But while he may not have been impressed with the view, he had become much more involved with me. Or was it me that had gotten more involved with him? The bottom line—one of the few my father failed to snort—is that we had both become increasingly involved with one another, finally and for the first time in our once strangely uninvolved lives.

Somewhere along this line I finally found that maybe I had to stop waiting around for him to give me something he probably didn't—at least not in any conventional sense—actually have to give. But, what if that turned out to be enough! Or how about if it were more than I could have ever imagined getting—especially given how low, bordering on nonexistent, my expectations actually were. But there I was, looking after him in those last however many years. I talked to his doctors, keeping in constant contact not only with him, but with his ever-changing, reliably constant rotation of Asian caregivers who not only rolled his joints, changed his jammies, administered his medication, and fed him his meals, but also routinely scrubbed the age lines that regularly creased his pale worn skin till it seemed to return to its former appearance of being both shiny and uncommonly smooth.

The ladies held on to both his watch and pinky ring for me

after they'd been removed following his recent unsuccessful surgery. And holding his ring in the flat of my hand, I remembered the square-shaped stone sparkle as he nervously gripped my upper arm as we stood dead center stage at the Berkeley Repertory Theatre, where I had been performing my show *Wishful Drinking.* On this particular evening my father had attended my show, accompanied by his two nurses Sarah and Augy, his dealer Randy (naturally), and his little dog Minnie. The audience applauded wildly as I stood beside my beaming father, his head hunched over and his left leg jiggling nervously. When the applause finally subsided, I leaned down to him and whispered, "Do you want to sing 'If I Loved You?' " I asked him this tentatively, with my shoulders scrunched up high, and he began to laugh, his eyes shining.

"Of course!" he replied enthusiastically.

So, I held my hand up in order to silence the cheering crowd and told them, "My dad and I are going to sing the song we always sang together, ever since I was a little girl. It's the song 'If I Loved You' from the show *Carousel.* " And as the audience's clapping and cheering once more subsided, I kneeled down next to him, my face upturned to his and, with his gaze fixed tightly to mine and after a hush no bigger than your fist, we began to sing—face to face, voice to voice, each wound round the other, father and daughter, two voices, no waiting, one song. My father, wheelchair-bound at my side, riding the song to the end of its harmonious journey. And as the last note slowly faded back to silence, the crowd rose to its feet as one, cheering. My father sat quite still, holding my hand, seemingly absorbing his ovation. Then he began oh so slowly to rise until he was standing upright, miraculously, as if he'd somehow been healed by show business. Raised up to the heavens, mobile, and in somehow perfect health. Whole again. The crowd had loved him till he was healthy, happy, and home free.

I wore the ring to his memorial, on the middle finger of my right hand. His send-off was a small affair attended by his three daughters, this one mournful ex-wife, and a couple of comics. The sad gathering was naturally held in the exclusive private back room of Factor's, a West Side deli located on Pico Boulevard. We all mingled beneath an array of photos of Eddie laughing with beautiful women or singing in clubs or on TV. My half sisters periodically snuck covetous looks at Eddie's ring glittering smugly on my hand, knowing on some secret level of the Fisher family language that it belonged to all of us, and that one day each of us would look down at our hands and there it would shine. "Oh, that's at least five or six karats," one untrained observer studying my stubby little hand told me, while another, looking doubtful, his brow furrowed seriously, volunteered, "I'd say it's ten, and I know my diamonds," prompting a third to say, "That thing is worth at *least* fifty grand, and I'm being conservative. I mean, who knows how much this thing could turn out to be worth?"

Well, it turned out that someone did. A few weeks after this, I not quite unexpectedly found myself doing my show in Australia, and one day, while shopping in one of their malls one afternoon in a jewelry shop specializing in fire opals, I suddenly thought, *Hey! Who better to appraise my dad's ring than a jeweler with one of those 10x magnifying eyepiece things?*

At first this particular jeweler hemmed and hawed awkwardly, a timid predator circling his distracted prey. As I watched, he turned the ring slowly, squinting at the stone, studying it carefully, turning it back and forth and back and forth. He finally spoke, still examining the gem in his hand. "This could be as much as ten karats," he offered. My eyes widened. I looked at my friend Garret, whose eyebrows also climbed northward toward his hairline and beyond to the blue Sydney skies.

Suddenly the jeweler's voice changed slightly. "Oooooh, wait. Hang on a tick," he suggested. And so we waited—I mean, really, what were our options? "I'm beginning to notice these . . . uh . . . what would they be? . . . little chips around the edge near the center, which . . . Well, if it were actually a diamond . . ." He lifted his head and gave me a look, a combination of concern, guilt, and apology. "Well, you see, if it were actually a diamond . . . there wouldn't be any chips is all." I hesitated, gradually absorbing this new information, and then I began slowly nodding, a smile spreading across my not-that-amazed face. Perfect. There you go. This totally made absolute Eddie Fisher sense. "Would you like to have a look?" the jeweler offered gently, holding his magnifying glass sympathetically toward me.

I held up the palm of my hand to convey my low level of

need to confirm that my father's ring turned out to not be the hoped-for legacy of not quite inestimable value, but was, instead, seven or eight karats of cubic zirconium.

The thing is, I loved my dad. I mean, the man was beyond fun to hang out with, appreciative, playful, and eccentrically sweet. He was all those things and a whole lot more, but this was also a man who—though he genuinely *meant* to give bona fide diamonds of only the finest color, cut, and clarity—ultimately was only able to offer cubic zirconium. But hey, a ring's a ring however you cut it, right? I mean, karats or no, the thing sparkles. The main thing is, finally, that my dad wore this ring for years and years and years until the end of his long lovable lunatic ride. So if you see any of my siblings, could *you* tell them about the ring not being real? I'm sorry, but I just can't seem to bring myself to break this one last, teeny bit of hilarious exciting news. Not that I think any of them will ultimately be any more surprised than I was. I mean, there is just something so perfect, so right, so *Eddie* about this news.

He came to me in a dream one night while I was in Sydney on tour Down Under, with my now one-and-a-half-woman show. It was the night before my birthday and, after watching an enjoyable documentary on serial murderers, I took my meds and drifted off to sleep. I dreamt my father was alive again and particularly wanted to let me know how pissed he was that I had his ring. Keeping my eye on the bigger picture here I said, "But we embalmed you! How could you have survived that?" I mean the man sounded *fantastic,* albeit pissed about how he'd been treated in death. Ringwise, that is. "Tell you what!" I said. "Next time write a fucking will that gives us ANY kind of instruction on what you want done! And who you want to do it!" Then I attempted to shift gears. Where were my manners? The man *was* back from the dead! "Wait till you see some of your obituaries! They were totally *awesome!* Seriously! I mean, there was even all this stuff about you knowing presidents and everything! Elizabeth Taylor even cried when I told her!"

Somehow, though, none of this alleviated his irritation. I told him how glad I was that he was alive. His death had upset me so much. Then I realized that all the people who had sent me their condolences would probably write me again, wanting the details on how he had outlived death. What was his secret? I called my half sisters, Joely and Trisha, to tell them, but they already knew—it had been on the news—and they were en route to see him at the house I had rented for him in Berkeley. I tried and tried but couldn't reach my brother, no matter what combination of numbers I employed. I wouldn't be able to go see him for a while, because I was in Australia doing my show, but I knew now that I would have to send him back his ring.

In his later years Eddie had come to realize that he was a very bad father (though, to his credit, unlike Harry, I don't think I ever heard him pass gas). His less than commendable paternal skills were never far from his mind, and you have to give him a lot of credit for acknowledging that. I know I do. I mean, he truly knew that any attention I gave him during the last few years of his life was not of a reciprocal nature. I was caring for him not because I was *expected* to but because I wanted to. Because he so enjoyed my visits that it was a pleasure to give them to him and my pleasure increased his even more. He appreciated being taken care of, and it was largely for that reason that I did it.

Essentially he truly understood that he'd really blown it with me—I mean blown it with all of his kids, but I like to think he regretted his lack of relationship with me the most. Not that that's necessarily true. It's just that it's never too late to want to be the favorite.

Near the end he was doing all he could to get to know me, everything from hugging me tighter than any man had ever hugged me in my life to calling me fifteen times a week. I mean, if when I was young, I had gotten even one of those calls a month, I would've been over the moon. I talked to him on the Fourth of July, a few months before he died, from Jackson Hole, Wyoming, where I was on vacation with a few friends, and I was telling him all the stuff we were doing—river rafting and fireworks and all this other cool stuff—and when I finished he said, "I wish I had your life." To which I replied, "You did, Daddy. That's why you're in bed." And the great thing was that he totally got it. It wasn't just something I was saying for my own amusement that whizzed over his head, and that I would tell my friends about later. My dad had a real sense of humor, and on top of that he had this huge appreciation for irony. He was packed to the gills with a hunger for fun.

FUNGER! The guy was loaded with it, that and especially in the end so, so much more.

When my father died, I lost something I never had. Something I sort of got in the bottom of the ninth. But by then things were reversed. I was the parent, to the point that sometimes he even called me Mommy.

But you know what? What was great was that if he loved you—and he truly did love me, maybe he especially loved me even more in his desperate state—he could make you feel that your world lit up brighter than any star, movie or otherwise. More than almost anything this was a joyous man, which is the thing I truly realized about him right in time to lose it. But at least I had it to lose. Which was for me, in the end, the thing. Ultimately I'm grateful that we connected at all. Because a little of him was a whole lot for me. Not really enough, of course, but a big bunch of something essential.

I did an interview recently where I was talking about, of all things, myself. And I said that sometimes I felt like I was more a persona than a person, designed more for public than private, and I illustrated this notion with the thing that Cary Grant famously said: "Everybody wants to be Cary Grant, even me." And the interviewer said, "Yeah, but no one really wants to be Carrie Fisher."

I mean, he said it in the nicest way possible, and I completely understood what he meant. "Well, you know, actually there is an area where you should want to be Carrie Fisher," I told him. Because there is something in me that is joyous, that's joyful. I don't hate hardly ever, and when I love, I love for miles and miles. A love so big it should either be outlawed or it should have a capital and its own currency.

And that, along with an unfortunate affinity for illegal substances and a diagnosis of manic depression, are among the many gifts bequeathed genetically by my father.

The man Eddie and I forged a relationship from common characteristics that most people don't actually covet and some of these characteristics were immaturity, forgetfulness, a perhaps unhealthy fondness for shopping (continuing to make purchases long past the point that we could afford to) and an enthusiasm for the altered state that bordered on suicidal. Not that we went to those lengths while in one another's company, but there was an unspoken understanding that we were willing to go to any lengths in our attempt to escape experiencing any and all intense and/or unwelcome feeling (i.e., the high) that's simply not otherwise inescapably low.

So this is what we shared in addition to brown eyes, good singing voices, and kidney stones. This is what we shared instead of a wealth of common experience and history. We shared a love for escape from reality, a sense that any reality one found oneself in could, and should, be improved. And for a long while, that was enough, perhaps because it had to be and partly because I finally realized that the way to have a satisfying, even fulfilling, certainly reliable and predictable relationship with my dad was for me to take care of him. To make him feel loved, appreciated and understood. To parent my parent was the pathway to my relationship with Eddie Fisher, my old Pa-pa. Enough of a relationship to where I miss him now. A lot. And I miss him in a very different way than how I missed him throughout my childhood.

Then I missed the idea of him. Now I miss the man—my dad.

Carrie Fisher, Eddie Fisher and Todd Fisher, nude from the waist down.

The last picture in the book.

Acknowledgments

I'd like to thank my dad for staying alive long enough for me to have a relationship worth savoring (but I can't thank him because he passed away).

I'd like to thank my mother—so I will! Thank you, Mama, I mean, who's a more bitchen parent than you, right? Seriously, there are no words. There are, however, a few dance moves.

Thanks to my brother Todd, his loyal cat,

my Uncle Bill, Trisha and Joely and their respective clan, which pretty much covers things on the immediate family front.

Thanks to Clancy Immusland for the years of keeping me so close to sanity, I can sometimes feel the breezes.

Thanks to Garret, my familiar, my memory and without whom I would be something—but the sum of that wouldn't be as high (but I might be).

Thanks to Gloria Grayton and Mary Douglas French, without whom I hope I'll never have to find out how close to nothing I'd be.

Thanks to my old, but not elderly, friend Paul Slansky, who's been known to save me from myself, or someone just as short.

And finally I'd like to thank my tribe: Bruce Wagner (for the title, for wanting to be a nurse, and for knowing what a lie is), Dave Mirkin (innovator of the "blurse" phenomenon—hybrid of blessing and curse), Cyndi Sayre (my souped-up new improved savior), Michael Tolkin, Wendy Mogel, Melissa North, Edgar and Rachel Phillips, Fred "the fixer" Bimbler, Roy Teeluck, Abe Gurko, Chas Weston, Michael Gonzales, Gale and Nikki Rich, Quinn Tivey, Nancy Braun, Teresa Crites, Kerry Jones, Dr. Jeff Wilkins, Dr. Barry Kramer, Bryan, Bruce & Ava, Penny, Bev, Sean, Salman, Melan, Max, G deB of Fee and Gee, Griplin, Helen, Nichols, Marcus, Graham, Ruby, Rufus, Buck, James B., Corby, Cynthia, Art, Merle, Carol, Steve, the Cohens, AWK &Co. and the Godchildren (James Goodman, Little Ed, Dash, Olivia and Anton), and my father's nurses: Sarah and Augie and everyone else from the far flung east.

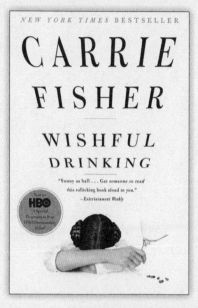